THE INTERPRETATION OF DREAMS

TOTEM AND TABOO
THREE ESSAYS ON THE THEORY OF SEXUALITY
AND OTHER WORKS

A CRITICAL COMMENTARY

ROBERT N. PASOTTI
ADELPHI UNIVERSITY

Macmillan General Reference
A Prentice Hall Macmillan Company
15 Columbus Circle
New York, NY 10023

ISBN: 0-671-00986-9

Printed in the United States of America

NOTE TO THE STUDENT

This Critical Commentary is designed to aid you in your comprehension and appreciation of Freudian theory. It will make little sense to you unless you are already familiar with a reputable edition of Freud's basic works. The author assumes, throughout his discussion, that this Commentary will prompt you to refer back to the original texts. A list of American editions of Freud, listed according to publisher, will be found in the Bibliography.

The Editors
Monarch Notes

TABLE OF CONTENTS

INTRODUCTION

In discouraging an attempt to abbreviate and summarize his works, Freud once remarked that he felt such undertakings usually deterred the reader from going to the original sources themselves and, at the same time, such abbreviated summaries deluded him into believing that he had obtained a sufficient grasp of the subject matter. The author trusts that such will not be the case with the present volume. The range, depth, and profundity of Freud's thought, the incalculable influence his discoveries have had in all areas of human understanding, and the sometimes tortured twistings and turnings, revisions and recantations that his theories underwent over a creative life which spanned almost half a century defy any attempt at a summary description. There is just too much there. Contrary to a popular misconception, Freud was not dogmatic. Many of his most important conclusions were put forth with the greatest tentativeness and, especially in some of his later works, his ideas often suffer from inconclusiveness and are even a little vague. Freud was a complete dualist and his theories sometimes seem to be expressions of his own personal ambivalence; that is, the inability (or refusal) to hold a single exclusive position and deny the truth of its opposite. This fact makes for a rich comprehensiveness but it also substantially contributes to the difficulties the beginner will find in the attempt to say clearly and with authority just what Freud's ideas were.

Varied and conflicting schools of psychology have grown out of the seeds which Freud so liberally scattered throughout his writings. (A student once observed that a Freudian footnote was often worth more than chapters by other psychologists.) And one of the principal tasks of this brief work will be the attempt to help clarify just what Freudian Psychoanalysis is, and just what it is not. A monumental confusion abounds in the minds of students and professionals alike in attempting to distinguish the principles of *Psychiatry* and *Psychotherapy*. These terms are often used with a great deal of imprecision as interchangeable, which they are not! As a brief working definition of Psychoanalysis, the author proposes the following: *Psychoanalysis is just what Freud says it is and nothing else.* He himself felt bitter about the appropriation of the term made by C. G. Jung and others and argued in the Introductory Lectures and elsewhere that since he had made the fundamental discoveries of this revolutionary science of the mind, he and he alone was entitled to say what doctrines comprised Psychoanalysis. The stupendous discoveries of the unconscious mind, the Oedipus Complex, the nature of dreams, the etiology of the neuroses, infantile sexuality, and the origin and meaning of civilization's most important institutions, religion, morality, the family, and art, plus the elaboration of a therapeutic technique which could uncover the most hidden recesses of the human psyche and alleviate the suffering of neurotically ill human beings, gave him the legitimate right, Freud argued, to demarcate the boundaries of the science of Psychoanalysis. Any psychology which claimed this august title for itself but at the same time denied the relevance of these discoveries simply was not Psychoanalysis.

His biographer Dr. Ernest Jones has written that Freud's discoveries must be studied chronologically in collaboration with a step-by-step discussion of the growth and changes in his personality. But for the purposes of this book the author feels that an intense concentration on Freud's discoveries and the books in which he discussed them is required. Freud identified three of his works as those which he took to be his most significant contribution to human knowledge: *The Interpretation of Dreams (Traumdeutung),*

Totem and Taboo, and *Three Essays on the Theory of Sexuality,* although there were other works which he personally preferred, the *Leonardo da Vinci* monograph for example. Dr. Jones added to this list the essay on the unconscious (1915). As a starting point, we shall concentrate on these four works (and their derivatives), the discoveries made in them, and correlate these with Freud's other major works which are extensions, confirmations, and sometimes rejections of the fundamental discoveries.

However, it must be noted that there exists an important break in the continuity of Freud's thoughts after 1920 when a novel and overriding discovery led him to posit the existence of what he termed a *Death Instinct (Todestrieb).* This discovery severely modified and in some ways contradicted his first theory concerning the nature of human instincts. The theory of the Death Instinct remains one of the most obscure and baffling hypotheses ever put forth by the father of Psychoanalysis.

The Three Categories

Our discussion will be divided into three major categories. This is not meant to imply the existence of any definitive lines of demarcation between Freud's *Clinical, Cultural* and *Metapsychological* theories. But his intellectual life did fall into three distinct periods within which his interests and discoveries tended to center on quite different areas of human activity. What we shall call the *"Clinical Period"* covers the years from 1895 to 1917 and slightly overlaps the beginnings of Freud's *"Cultural Period"* which extends from 1913 to the end of his life in 1939. The *"Metapsychological Period"* comprises the years 1920-1939 and is initiated by the highly speculative essay, *Beyond the Pleasure Principle.* But these distinctions are more a matter of literary convenience than descriptive of radical breaks in the Freudian chain of thought. Freud wrote clinical, cultural, and metapsychological books and papers throughout his life.

Clinical

We use the term *Clinical* to describe all those discoveries Freud made in the actual practice of Psychoanalysis as a branch of medicine. The major works of this period are: *The Interpretation of Dreams* (1900), *Three Essays on the Theory of Sexuality* (1905), *Studies in Hysteria* (1895), and *The Psychopathology of Everyday Life* (1901). Without question, *A General Introduction to Psychoanalysis* (a series of lectures which Freud delivered in the years 1915-1917 to the Medical Faculty of the University of Vienna), and the last book he wrote and never completed, *An Outline of Psychoanalysis* (1939), present the beginning student with the very finest available summary of the principles of Psychoanalysis.

Cultural

The *Cultural Period* in the history of Psychoanalysis begins with the publication of *Totem and Taboo* in 1913, and signifies the application of Freud's clinical techniques and discoveries to the problems of civilization. *Group Psychology and the Analysis of the Ego* (1921), and *Moses and Monotheism* (1939), will also be discussed.

Metapsychological

The term *Metapsychological* will perhaps be unfamiliar to most readers. By his own admission Freud struggled throughout his life with a strong inclination toward philosophical speculation. In the early years of the great clinical discoveries he confessed that he had forcibly mastered this tendency but with the writing of *Totem and Taboo,* which by its very nature defies any attempt at clinical verification, Freud relented, and permitted himself the luxury of going far beyond the range of empirical evidence. Finally, in the last two decades of his life (1920-1939), his distaste for "non-scientific" speculation vanishes, and we find him grappling with the eternal philosophic problems of life and death, the essence of man, the relationship between freedom and determinism, and what came to be his overriding concern, "How did human nature get to be what it is?" In his own words, he permitted himself to "give free rein" to his speculative tendencies. Our inquiry into Freudian Metapsychology will lead us to examine the three major works of this period, *Beyond the Pleasure Principle, The Future of an Illusion,* and *Civilization and Its Discontents.*

We may thus distinguish two broad general tendencies in the development of Psychoanalysis, the practical and the theoretical: Psychoanalysis as therapy, the attempt to alleviate the suffering of neurotically ill human beings, and Psychoanalysis as theory, i.e., cultural and metapsychological speculation. As time went on, Freud became convinced that his great achievement would finally be recognized not so much for its medical value as a curative agent in the field of mental disease, but rather as a tool of cultural investigation and explanation which would shed light on the hitherto obscure realms of the beginnings of the institutions of human culture.

Freud was convinced that the understanding of so-called "abnormal" mental activity, neurosis, psychosis, the perversions, as well as the minor errors and accidents which fill our daily lives and the strangely familiar yet till then incomprehensible realm of dreams, would provide a unifying clue to a comprehensive theory and law of mental functioning. This is what Metapsychology attempts, the unification and explanation of all the elements of human psychology, conscious-unconscious, normal-abnormal, individual-social, intellectual-emotional, an ambitious project which Freud felt he had only begun.

Psychoanalysis: An Intellectual Revolution

Freud considered himself one of the discoverers who had "wakened the human race from its slumbers," and contributed to the dethroning of man as the central figure in the universe. The first modern thinker in the Western tradition to accomplish this was the Polish mathematician Nicholas Copernicus who initiated the cosmological revolution of the seventeenth century by mathematically establishing (in his *De Revolutionibus Orbium Coelestium* [*On the Revolutions of the Heavenly Spheres*], 1543) the heliocentric theory of the universe, the now thoroughly accepted fact that the earth revolves around the sun and is not the fixed center of a universe singled out by a beneficent Deity for special consideration among all the heavenly bodies. The earth was no longer special. Then, in 1859, Charles Darwin dealt the human ego its second great blow by propounding the Theory of Evolution (no longer considered a theory but rather the foundation of modern biology). In place of the traditional religious contention that man was an act of special creation and different in essence from the lower animals by virtue of his possession of an immortal soul, Darwin amassed a convincing amount of evidence to demonstrate that man is completely a product of natural forces, sharing a much closer kinship to nature's animals than God's angels. Man and the primates share a common ancestry and their specific differences can be thoroughly explained by the natural mechanisms of physical evolution.

In several places Freud wrote that he had dealt the final lethal stroke to human ignorance and arrogance by demonstrating that man's behavior, seemingly guided by conscious motives, seemingly free, and seemingly rational (Greek philosophy had defined man as the "rational animal"), was on the contrary the product of powerful unconscious, determined, and irrational energies of whose very existence he was unaware, and over which he exercised little or no control. Freud employed the metaphor of an iceberg to describe how human consciousness is grounded in the unconscious (significantly, Freud termed the operation of the unconscious the *Primary Process*). Only a small portion of an iceberg is visible, the rest is hidden from sight. But it is the invisible portion of the iceberg, by far the greatest portion of it, which determines and directs its movements. So it is with human behavior. By far the greater portion of the human psyche is invisible, i.e., unconscious, and yet it is the unconscious which determines (not just influences but *"determines"*) the apparently consciously directed, free, rational manifestations of human behavior.

Specificity of Freud's "Unconscious"

But it was not simply Freud's assertion that unconscious elements play a much bigger role in human behavior than generally believed that startled and outraged his contemporaries. The nineteenth century in Europe produced a number of philosophies which argued for the pre-eminence of non-rational energies in the human mind. Schopenhauer, Nietzsche, Von Hartmann and others had structured their philosophies on just such an assertion. It was the Freudian discovery of the *specific nature* of the *Primary Process* that once and for all put an end to the illusion of the supremacy of *conscious, rational,* and especially *moral* agents motivating and determining human behavior. For the unconscious is the repository of all those impulses, purposes, wishes and drives which civilized man reserves to animal and savage behavior, and from which he invariably excuses himself. Murderous impulses, incestuous wishes, sadism, cannibalism, sexual perversions and boundless egoism dominate the human unconscious, and exercise profound and far-reaching influences on our conscious behavior which seems so far removed from them. Civilized man was discovered to be first and foremost an animal who had never relinquished his primitive sexual and aggressive drives, although he had become a past master at distinguishing them to himself and creating rationalizations to apologize for his most blatant behavioral contradictions of the principles of consciousness, rationality and morality.

Sexual Discoveries and Responses

It was the discovery of the universality of sex and aggression in every manifestation of human behavior that brought down on Freud the condemnation of his contemporaries. And although his name has become a household word today, his discoveries viewed with admiration in wide areas of our intellectual culture and his therapeutic technique still forming the backbone of Psychoanalysis, there exists a convincing body of evidence to indicate that, as Freud himself remarked on the occasion of his seventieth birthday, the world has adopted Psychoanalysis simply in order to be better able to destroy it! If this is so, civilized man has not yet come to grips with his unconscious, nor can he tolerate the discoveries of a great scientist who first brought him face to face with the unpalatable truth about himself.

Nothing surprised Freud more than the ridicule and vehemence with which the lay and medical world of the late nineteenth century rejected his well-documented discoveries. One critic accused Freud of being an immoral man living in the immoral atmosphere of that immoral city, Vienna. Another suggested that he had corrupted the innocence of the nursery. (The specific details of this kind of "criticism" will be dealt with in a later chapter.) Freud was a man of strong moral sentiments, unimpeachable behavior, a highly developed sense of honesty, and an almost constitutional distrust of instinctual behavior. He was possessed of what we may term the highest scientific integrity and respect for facts, both those that confirmed and those that might conceivably refute his discoveries. All he asked was that colleagues and critics alike examine his findings, not his character.

For example, to Freud it was obvious, and easily verifiable in the nursery, that the infant is an animal dominated by egoism and propelled by sexual and aggressive drives surpassing even those of an adult. But it was well-nigh impossible for his Victorian contemporaries to accept or even consider this fact. Freud held no illusions on that score. But what did shock and dismay him at first was the tone of utterly unscientific, personal invective directed at him *(n.b., not at the evidence)* by the medical, professional, theological and lay communities. It was as if he had created the repellent aspects of human psychology rather than honestly and openly discussing them with total scientific objectivity.

Gradually Freud realized, as he put it, that the world did not give thanks to those who revealed the nature and importance of sexuality in human affairs. But it was not until his discovery of the *Resistances* in psychoanalytic therapy that he could comprehend why these assaults had been so vicious, irrelevant to what he had discovered, and personal.

Freudian Terminology

In beginning the study of any science, philosophy, or foreign language, it is essential that the student comprehend the vocabulary of that particular discipline. The vocabulary of Psychoanalysis is no exception. Freud created a substantial number of new terms and concepts in order to better describe the unfamiliar subject matter of his revolutionary science of the mind. But he did not always use his terms with mathematical precision (by the very nature of the subject matter this would have been an impossible task) and, as his own knowledge of depth-psychology increased, earlier concepts developed far-reaching and at times, entirely novel connotations. The glossary of the essential terms to be found in the body of the text on page 156 is meant simply to function as an outline. These are the basic elements of the Freudian vocabulary, the grammar and syntax so to speak, the bare bones which take on meaningful flesh only when the entire text has been read.

PART ONE

THE CLINICAL PERIOD (1895-1913)

A. The Major Works

1. *The Interpretation of Dreams* (1900)
2. *Three Essays on the Theory of Sexuality* (1905)
3. *The Psychopathology of Everyday Life* (1901)
4. *Studies in Hysteria* (1895)

B. Later works which unify, clarify and correct these major works

1. *A General Introduction to Psychoanalysis* (1915-1917)
2. *An Outline of Psychoanalysis* (1939)

This study guide will divide Freud's writings into three distinct but often overlapping periods: the *Clinical* (1895-1913), the *Cultural* (1913-1939), and the *Metapsychological* (1920-1939). But before proceeding to a detailed analysis of these writings, it will be necessary to further develop our preliminary definition of *Psychoanalysis,* and distinguish it from *Psychology, Psychiatry,* and *Psychotherapy.*

Psychology

By the generic term *Psychology* is meant any theory or body of knowledge dealing with the human psyche. Psyche is a Greek word which means the "soul," but not necessarily soul in the religious or supernatural context with which English-speaking students are familiar; that is, an insubstantial, immortal thing which survives bodily death. The Greeks meant two things by the term psyche: First, a principle of motion, anything that "moved" had a soul. Now by defining psyche as that which moved anything they meant, in addition to simply locomotion (movement from place to place), growth, decay, change of quality, and in general any energetic process observable by the five senses. The second connotation given by the ancients to the word psyche was: *Principle of Life.* Anything that lived possessed a psyche. Hence, plants and animals had souls and so did the heavenly bodies, the stars, planets and constellations. The suffix "logos" (psyche-logos) means the inquiry into, the study of, or the essence or nature of anything. The compound word Psychology thus translates into the study (and knowledge) of the human soul, essence, nature, or what is perhaps a more congenial term, personality. Psychology studies and gives knowledge of the human personality. *Psychoanalysis* is a psychology. But Freud adopted a term first employed by C. G. Jung, *Depth Psychology,* in order to differentiate Psychoanalysis from all other psychologies. The use of this term applied to Psychoanalysis implies that all other psychologies are "superficial," that is, they deal with observable, consciously reported data about human behavior and do not go below the surface. Freud did not contrast depth-psychology with "superficial-psychology" in any derogatory sense. He simply meant that traditional psychologies of consciousness, such as the psychology of Wilhelm Wundt, perhaps the most influential of Freud's contemporaries, did not go deep enough into the nature of the psyche and did not employ the hard-won techniques and discoveries of Psychoanalysis. They did not and could not deal with that portion of *the iceberg* hidden from view. So that while *Psychoanalysis* is most definitely a *Psychology,* a theory of human personality, this by no means implies that all psychologists are committed to the theory and practice of *Psychoanalysis.*

Psychiatry

The term *Psychiatry* is often identified with *Psychoanalysis.* This is most emphatically *not* correct. One of the raging controversies which surrounded Freud in the 1920's was whether the practice of *Lay Analysis* was either possible or desirable. By *Lay Analysis* is meant the ability of a non-physician to practice *Psychoanalysis*. Must a man be a medically licensed physician in order to be a psychoanalyst? Freud's answer was a definite No. *Psychiatry* is a branch of physical medicine. Its practice *requires* a medical degree. The psychiatrist employs medical devices which the psychoanalyst may not (unless he is at the same time a licensed physician) employ, i.e., drugs, shock treatment, surgical intervention, etc. Freud himself *was* a licensed physician as were most of the early adherents to Psychoanalysis. But he argued most emphatically that Psychoanalysis was *not* exclusively a branch of medicine, and that laymen (non-physicians) could practice it as well as, if not better than, medically-licensed psychiatrists who had not been trained in its special techniques and theories.

Psychotherapy

Psychotherapy is a general and diffuse term. There exist literally dozens of kinds of psychotherapy which pay no attention whatever to Freud's theories and methods. Psychoanalysis is a particular kind of psychotherapy, but it is not equivalent to psychotherapy in general. The followers of Jung, Adler, Rodgers, Horney, T. Reik and many others practice psychotherapy, that is, the attempt to relieve the suffering of the emotionally disturbed. But the essence of *Psychoanalysis* as a kind of *Psychotherapy* is its total commitment to the existence and overriding importance of UNCONSCIOUS MENTAL PROCESSES. And the key to an understanding of these processes is to be found in the interpretation of dreams. It is now time to dissect dreams and lay bare their anatomy.

"The Interpretation of Dreams" (1900)

The cornerstone of Psychoanalysis is the interpretation of dreams. Freud called dream-interpretation the *via reggia*, the "royal road" to the unconscious, and it is the theory of dreams that has best stood the test of time over a period of more than seventy years.

Freud admired Aristotle's dictum that dreaming is the activity of the mind during sleep. It was perhaps the use of the term activity that Freud most appreciated in this brief definition for, as his understanding of the dynamics of dreaming increased, so did the impression of ceaseless mental activity differing in quality from that of ordinary waking life. In fact, the quality of mental activity during sleep differed so radically from what we take to be the essence of mental functioning that Freud coined the term "Kingdom of the Illogical" to describe that realm of the human psyche which the technique of dream-interpretation allowed him to penetrate.

Dreams in History

The idea that dreams possess meaning was certainly not new with Freud; indeed, it has been held since the very beginnings of the Western intellectual tradition. In Chapter 3 of Homer's *Iliad*, Zeus sends a dream to the Greek king Agamemnon which requires interpretation and leads to a renewed assault on Troy. We are all familiar with the dream interpretations in the Old Testament. Perhaps the best known of these interpretations is the one delivered by Joseph to the Pharaoh of Egypt. Joseph's interpretation of the Pharaoh's dreams was so accurate that he was rewarded by being made prime minister of Egypt. The therapeutic use of dream-interpretation was also known to the ancients. At the temple of Asclepius in Epidaurus, Greek physician-priests required their patients to sleep one night on the porch of the temple and then report their dreams to them before diagnosis and treatment would be undertaken. And we are all familiar with cheap dream-interpretation books to be found in the five-and-ten cent store and the popular newspaper columns dealing with the same subject. Humanity has always taken its dreams quite seriously.

Two important facets of Freud's mind are revealed in his approach to dreams. First, he always took as meaningful any widely held beliefs, any enduring tradition, and any values and actions which had survived the test of historical time. Simply because beliefs, traditions, values and actions had survived was reason enough for studying them as sources of the enduring mental qualities of humanity. The materialistic science (and psychology) of the nineteenth century dismissed dreams as mental waste products without meaning or importance, but for Freud, ALL MANIFESTATIONS OF HUMAN BEHAVIOR, THE MOST TRIVIAL AS WELL AS THE MOST UNINTELLIGIBLE, could provide clues to an understanding of human psychology. This Freudian conviction was to become the first law of psychoanalytic theory, the principle of *psychic determinism*. All behavior has a *cause* which *determines* its *nature*. There exist no random, accidental, nonsensical or uncaused events in the science of Psychoanalysis. Where dreams were viewed as meaningless mental excrescences, Freud took them seriously.

A second element of Freud's scientific personality emerges from his discussion of dreams. Throughout his life he always gave credit to those anticipations of Psychoanalysis that he found in the great writers and thinkers who had preceded him. He praised the German philosopher Arthur Schopenhauer for having anticipated by half a century the existence of the unconscious and the determining power it exercised upon consciouness, as well as Schopenhauer's keen intuitions of the omnipresence of sexuality in human affairs. Friedrich Nietzsche was another German thinker whom Freud singled out for special praise (indeed, Freud was to borrow Nietzsche's term ID, as definitive of the activities of the unconscious). Freud wrote that Nietzsche "knew himself better than any man who ever lived." The essential technique of psychoanalytic therapy to be discussed shortly, the technique of FREE ASSOCIATION, had actually been discovered by a popular writer, and Freud credited his contemporary Joseph Popper-Lynkaeus, a physicist, with having divined the crucial function of censorship-distortion in dreams. Dr. Joseph Breuer was generously acknowledged as something of a spiritual father of Psychoanalysis, and in a number of his writings Freud spoke with admiration of the philosopher Plato's two-thousand-year-old anticipations of some of his major discoveries, especially the theory of *Sublimation*. He always gave credit where it was due and sincerely admired the intuitions of the great creative artists: Shakespeare, Sophocles, Dostoyevsky, Goethe, and many more who so clearly understood the wellsprings of human action, an understanding which he himself arrived at only after decades of the most laborious scientific investigation.

"Insight such as this falls to one's lot but once in a lifetime." Thus Freud described his most important contribution to mental science, *The Interpretation of Dreams*. The book was begun, significantly enough, in 1896, the year of his father's death, an event he described as the most significant one in every man's life. At that time Freud's theory of sexuality was "not yet in existence," though impressive hints of the connection between unconscious sexuality and conscious behavior had been vouchsafed him both in his medical practice and in the writing of *Studies in Hysteria*. As late as 1931 Freud wrote of the *Interpretation of Dreams* that it contained the most valuable discoveries he had ever made, a significant modification of the generally held notion that sexuality alone was the field in which Freud had made his key discoveries. Typically, in the first chapter of his masterpiece, he exhaustively reviewed the scientific literature on dreams, and at the conclusion of the book, he remarked that only two of all previous theories could be totally excluded from his own: First, that dreams are meaningless; second, that they are purely the consequence of physical stimuli. All others were at least partially incorporated in his own revolutionary theory. Freud's rejection of the theory of the meaninglessness of dreams will emerge during the body of our discussion in this chapter. As for the belief that dreams are simply responses to either external, physical or internal physiological stimuli, i.e., the ticking of a clock in the sleeper's room, street noises outside the window, excessive heat or cold in the room, etc., or hunger, thirst, the need to excrete, or internal discomfort of any kind, Freud argued that it can be demonstrated that these stimuli provide only the *superficial cue* to the activity of dreaming, but not the *form and content* (the *Dream-Work* and the *Dream-Thoughts*) which the dream takes. The dream is by no means a passive response to external or internal stimuli. Rather, it is the active reworking of these stimuli for its own purposes that manifests the true nature of the dream.

A second popular view held that dreams are nocturnal responses to significant events of the preceding day (I meet an old friend during the day and then dream of him that night), and we shall see that Freud takes this account more seriously than the physical one. But again, it is the unique manner in which the Dream-Work elaborates what Freud calls the "residues" of the previous day's activities and encounters that cannot be accounted for except in terms of logic of the unconscious mind.

Dreams — A Freudian Definition

Superficially, we are all convinced that we know just what a "dream" is. But the most cursory investigation into the dream's essence suggests that after describing it as a "mental something which we have while sleeping," and perhaps, in accord with experiments currently being carried out in connection with the physiological concomitants of dreaming, Rapid-Eye Movements (REM), the various stages and depths of dream activity as reflected in changing rates of our vital signs (pulse-rate, heart-beat, brain-waves), and the time of the night when various kinds of dreams occur, we come up against what the philosopher Immanuel Kant called the *Ding-An-Sich* (thing-in-itself), and find ourselves unable to penetrate further into the hidden nature of this universal human experience.

The simple questions *what is a dream, how is it made* and *what is its purpose or meaning (if any)* gave birth to Freud's lengthiest and most important work in which he solved the riddle of the dream and supplied mental science with the techniques by which dreams can be interpreted and their meanings revealed.

Interpretation

The first point to be noted is this: if dreams must be "interpreted" obviously then they DO NOT MEAN what they seem to mean on the surface; the meaning of the dream (Dream-Thoughts) cannot be known by simply examining the contents of the dream itself (Manifest Dream). If dreams do not mean what they seem to mean then HOW do we arrive at their meaning? A deeper significance to dreaming then appears when we ask the next logical question, WHY don't dreams mean what they seem to mean (if they mean anything at all), and what could be the purpose of altering the real meaning? Why is it necessary? And HOW is this posited alteration in the meaning of dreams carried out and by what mental agency?

ALL DREAMS POSSESS MEANING. They are tendentious, purposeful, and there cannot be found any element in any dream no matter how apparently nonsensical or insignificant which can negate this first principle of dream-interpretation. ALL DREAMS POSSESS MEANING.

ALL DREAMS ARE *WISH-FULFILLMENTS*. ALL DREAMS (AS WELL AS *ALL* MANIFESTATIONS OF OBSERVABLE BEHAVIOR) ARE *COMPROMISE-FORMATIONS*. THE PURPOSE OF DREAMS IS TO MAINTAIN SLEEP. The corollaries to these major axioms of dream-interpretation are: The fulfilled wish will be of a definite kind; as is the case with all compromises, the Compromise-Formation in dreams will occur between opposing tendencies which go to make up the material of the dream, i.e., the specific kind of wishes and the maintenance of sleep must be shown to follow from the activity of dreaming.

In summary it may be stated that:

1. All dreams mean something.

2. The meaning of the dream is not evident in the dream itself.

3. Something happens to change the dream-meaning. HOW and WHY this occurs are crucial points.

4. There must be specifically discoverable mechanisms which reveal how dreams are made.

5. The process of dream-interpretation will enable us to uncover (or recover) the dream's true meaning. If Freud is correct, the interpretation of dreams will lay bare the true nature of unconscious mental activity.

Before entering into a detailed discussion of the afore-mentioned problems and deductions, a pertinent observation of Freud's concerning dream-interpretation, and by exten-sion, the whole of Psychoanalysis itself, must be examined. The art or science of dream-interpretation only becomes convincing when carried out on *ONE'S OWN DREAMS!* The discoveries of Psychoanalysis can only become con-vincing when applied to *one's own behavior*. On these points Freud remained adamant. Psychoanalysis cannot really be learned from books or lectures, it can only be learned "upon oneself." Perhaps these pronouncements sound arbitrary and dictatorial, a charge often levelled at Freud. But we can draw a helpful analogy between the process of learning a foreign language, and "learning" Psychoanalysis and the language of dream-interpretation. No one is equipped to rationally judge the greatness of an author who writes a language foreign to us if one has not taken the time to learn that language. In the learning of that language, of course, innumerable mistakes, misinterpretations, and misjudg-ments will occur. Material that is easily intelligible to a native speaker sounds like jibberish to the novice foreigner. Yet theoretically, the foreigner can come to understand the meaning of this "jibberish," and convert the once unintelligible sounds and symbols into meaningful discourse. But first, he must learn the meanings attached to certain symbols, the grammar and syntax, the idioms, the vocabulary, and even the argot of that language. IN EVERY WAY this process is comparable to acquiring a comprehension of the LANGUAGE OF THE UNCONSCIOUS AS SPOKEN IN DREAMS.

As anyone who has undertaken the task of learning a strange tongue knows, it is not acquired in classrooms or from books or the listening to records, but rather, is learned by and through oneself speaking that language and being corrected by those who speak it more fluently, i.e., like a native. This is the substance of Freud's dictum that dream-interpretation is learned upon (not BY) oneself. The vocabulary, grammar and syntax of dream-speech may be given us by a native speaker. But it is only through constant practice and use that we learn to understand and employ the language for ourselves.

For the beginning student the best introduction to Freud's theory of dreams remains the lectures he delivered to the faculty of the School of Medicine of the University of Vienna over the winter terms 1915-1917. (In fact the best general outline of the whole of Psychoanalysis is to be found there.) Some minor modifications of the dream theory appear in the *New Introductory Lectures to Psychoanalysis,* published in 1933, and the more than half-dozen revised editions of *The Interpretation of Dreams* issued during Freud's lifetime. The principal point for the student to keep in mind, however, is that the theory of dreams underwent the last change of all his theories from 1900-1939, and that the following discussion, culled from all of Freud's writings on the dream, represents an accurate and complete summary of his theories.

Essence of Dream Theory

Freud analyzes the dream into the following components which represent a blueprint of his theory:

1. An *unconscious wish* which is the true motivating power for the formation of the dream.

2. The *rejection of the unconscious wish* by a certain agency in consciousness which Freud terms the Censor. However, it is absolutely essential to remember that the act of censorship in dream-formation is NOT CONSCIOUS. This first paradox of Freudian thought is not fully explained until the fully matured theory of the unconscious-repressed ego and the pre-conscious which will be discussed later on.

3. The *Compromise-Formation* (between unconscious wish and its rejection) which allows the Dream-Work to carry out its principal purpose, the maintenance of sleep. It is to be henceforth sharply underlined that ALL conscious behavior, normal as well as neurotic, sleeping as well as waking, individual as well as cultural is cast in the form of Compromise-Formation.

4. The methods and techniques employed by the Censor (the Dream-Work) for distorting hence disguising the unconscious wish so that it may become acceptable to consciousness and achieve hallucinatory satisfaction in the dream.

5. The examination of the logic of "Kingdom of the Illogical," i.e., the unconscious as revealed in dreams.

6. The "kinds" of wishes fulfilled in dreams (why forbidden?).

7. If dreams are wish-fulfillments guarding sleep, why then do we often experience painful dreams, anxiety dreams and nightmares? These dreams often cause us to awaken instead of insuring sleep. How can wish-fulfillments and anxiety dreams be reconciled?

8. Dreams and dream wishes are universal (as well as the laws of mental functioning which they disclose), i.e., common to all men in all times and all places.

Manifest and Latent Dreams

Since most dreams contradict the laws of contradiction, as well as the laws of physical reality, it is not difficult to grasp the fact that their meaning must be hidden behind the facade of what we dream if they are to be made intelligible in the context of our waking experience. The first distinction Freud made in his theory was between what he called the *Manifest Dream,* just what it is we are dreaming in a particular dream, the content, the subject matter of that dream, and the *Latent Dream* or *Dream-Thoughts* which stand as the true purpose and meaning of the dream. The *Manifest Dream* must be unravelled like a puzzle or a riddle so that we can arrive at the dream's meaning, the *Dream-Thoughts* contained in the *Latent Dream.* This is the function of dream-analysis.

Dream-Work

But between the unconscious wishes which constitute the meaning of the *Latent Dream,* and the *Manifest Dream* itself, something takes place which alters the dream's meaning so that it appears in consciousness as a *disguised* wish. This intervening activity Freud called the *Dream-Work,* and it was his investigations into the nature of the *Dream-Work* that first brought the realms of unconscious and conscious psychology into an intelligible relationship with each other and laid the foundations for his further explorations and discoveries.

In the first formulation of the nature of *Dream-Work* Freud argued that it derives from a mental agency called the *Censorship,* which guards the accesses to consciousness and motility, and either prevents potentially disturbing unconscious wishes from becoming conscious, or so distorts and disguises them that they are no longer recognizable as *forbidden, anti-social, or immoral.* A fuller discussion of the nature of the *Censorship* must be postponed until we encounter Freud's mature theory of the *Super-Ego.* For the moment it is sufficient that the student grasp the concept of *Censorship* (disguise-distortion) as the principal mechanism of the *Dream-Work.*

Censorship

Since the *Censorship* is continuously at work during sleep, preventing some unconscious wishes and impulses from entering consciousness or only permitting them access to the *Manifest Dream* in a disguised and distorted form, the implication is clear that the unconscious wishes and impulses are not only unacceptable to consciousness but must be of such a nature that:

1. They are not conscious in the waking life of the dreamer. He is unaware of their existence when not dreaming.

2. A considerable amount of mental energy must be employed in preventing these wishes from entering consciousness. (Somehow, the Censorship operates to suppress them.)

3. They are so repellent to our customary, moral, consciously-avowed sensibilities that they would threaten the very purpose of the dream, the preservation of sleep, if allowed entry into consciousness undisguised or undistorted.

Yet, in some vague and unspecified way, the Censor *IS AWARE* of the existence and nature of the forbidden impulses and wishes; hence, Freud is led to the paradoxical assertion that the dreamer KNOWS the latent meaning of his dream, and yet he DOESN'T KNOW THAT HE KNOWS! Dream-interpretation and the whole of Psychoanalysis thus becomes a species of recollection and re-education!

Theoretically, the psychoanalyst knows the meaning of his patient's dream; thus, it would seem that all he need do would be to TELL the dreamer the meaning of his Manifest Dream in terms of its latent wish-fulfillment. This procedure, however, produces absolutely no conviction in the patient's mind and he tends to reject the analyst's interpretations. (It is worthwhile to remember that an unconscious process of censorship which endeavors to disguise the dream's true meaning from the dreamer is constantly at work in both the sleeping and waking states.) How then can the dreamer ever recollect what he knows when he does not know he knows and cannot be told so by the analyst?

It is important to recall that Freud based Psychoanalysis on the principle of *Psychological Determinism,* the principle that all mental events as well as all physical events are to be understood in terms of the strictest causality. Every piece of conscious behavior has an unconscious determining cause.

From this perspective Freud was able to draw the momentous conclusion that the patient himself can arrive at the dream's hidden meaning by supplying the CONNECTING LINKS between the unconscious Dream-Thoughts and the conscious Manifest Dream. The process of supplying these missing links between unconscious and conscious thoughts Freud called FREE ASSOCIATION.

Free Association

Although *Free Association* becomes the major instrument in undoing the distortions of the Censorship, leading to the meaning of the dream, the term is altogether misleading since *Free Association* is NOT FREE at all. Every association brought up in the analysis of dreams is causally linked in some way, no matter how distant or far-fetched, to the underlying meaning of the dream. The dreamer's associations are just as rigidly *determined causally* as any other conscious mental event, and if the chain of connecting links

is carefully scrutinized it will inevitably lead to the unconscious Dream-Thoughts.

Originally, in dealing with nervous disorder, Freud employed the technique of hypnosis. (This technique will be
fully discussed in the section below dealing with Hysteria.)
But hypnosis proved unsatisfactory as a therapeutic device,
principally because the patient DID NOT REMEMBER, in
the waking state, the material which had been recollected
under hypnosis. Consequently, the remission of neurotic
symptoms was at best temporary. In working out the method of *Free Association,* it slowly but convincingly dawned
on Freud that his patients could be led to an understanding
of their symptoms and dreams if they would undertake to
practice the principle of complete honesty. Freud called this
principle *THE ANALYTIC COMPACT.* By the Analytic
Compact. Freud meant that each patient (dreamer) must
voluntarily suspend all critical faculties and permit *ANY
THOUGHT,* no matter how seemingly irrelevant, repulsive,
silly, or unacceptable to appear in consciousness and be ver-
balized. Then, the patient (dreamer) is required to permit
ANY associated ideas whatsoever to appear in consciousness and then report them to the analyst. Psychoanalysis is
based upon the conviction that not just any unrelated idea
will present itself to the dreamer, but rather, that a casually
determined chain of associated ideas which will lead to the
true (Latent) meaning of the dream *must* appear. No matter how apparently irrelevant, nonsensical, repulsive, or
unacceptable this chain of associations may be to the dreamer's conscious mind, they must be reported to the analyst.
If the Analytic Compact can be honored by the patient,
Freud was convinced that the dream's meaning can be arrived at by the DREAMER HIMSELF, with some guidance
from the analyst. But this analytic assistance should never
take the form of "telling" the dreamer the meaning of his
dream. In fact, this is not possible since the dreamer does
not accept the interpretation given him. The analyst's primary function is to see to it that the dreamer remains hon-

est and adheres to the Analytic Compact by reporting ALL of his associations. In this manner the process of Free Association can unravel the distortions of the Dream-Work (Censorship), and recover the unconscious Dream-Thoughts. This is the essence of psychoanalytic therapy.

Symbolism and Man

In his discovery of "how" the Censorship operates in dreams, Freud revealed one of the most archaic and universal features of the human mind, an activity to be found not only in dreaming but in the creation of the world's great mythologies, fairy tales, art, humor, psychotic delusions, etc., and this discovery convinced him that in understanding how to correctly interpret the dream he had at the same time deepened our comprehension of the dynamics of these other creations. Freud spoke of the ARCHAIC nature of dreams, meaning by this that dreams employ techniques and methods in their activity which enlighten us on the most ancient and primitive modes of mental functioning. The principal element in our ARCHAIC HERITAGE is the activity of SYMBOLISM.

Symbolism is to be found in all human cultures and all human activities. Freud gave no esoteric definition of Dream-Symbolism. He meant by it just what the ordinary layman would mean; elements in the Manifest Dream (*what* we are dreaming) represent or stand for other elements in the Latent Dream (Dream-Thoughts). The activity of Dream-Symbolism is one of the principal ways in which the Censor works to disguise and distort the unconscious wish which is father to the conscious dream. ALL DREAMS ARE WISH-FULFILLMENTS, though often of a very peculiar kind. Freud defines the Dream-Work as "the replacement of a demand (instinctual) by the fulfillment of a wish." But if the function of dreaming is to preserve sleep, how then can we "wish" to wake up, as often happens in anxiety dreams or nightmares, and why are dreams so often unpleasant to the dreamer though he does not awaken? Does the dreamer wish to suffer in his dreams?

Paradoxes in Wish-Fulfillments

Now while the purpose of the Dream-Work is the preservation of sleep through the disguised fulfillment of unconscious wishes, IT DOES NOT ALWAYS SUCCEED in doing so. Anxiety dreams represent the failure of the Dream-Work to carry out its natural task and we awaken. Also, while one part of the mental personality (the unconscious) wishes to discharge its accumulated wishes, another part (the Censor) wishes to gain control over unconscious excitations and bind them. The result is often a compromise between the two systems in which opposing wishes are reconciled as well as they can be, and the dreamer maintains sleep. Often, dreaming seeks to gain control retrospectively over the memory of experiences which were not successfully concluded in the dreamer's past, and especially his childhood. Dream-Wishes are then of an INFANTILE AND REGRESSIVE nature. The wish, Freud writes, MUST BE INFANTILE in nature. Punishment dreams also exist, in which a third part of the mental anotomy (which Freud later termed *Super-Ego*) seems to fulfill the need to alleviate the *unconscious sense of guilt* which he discovered to be a crucial factor in human psychology. We often *unconsciously* wish for punishment, and this kind of dream fulfills that wish. With these qualifications of the nature of the Dream-Wish, Freud wrote that the theory of dreams "remained intact."

But the theory of dream symbolism takes the investigator far beyond the individual dreamer's personal past to the historical genesis of the thought-processes of the WHOLE HUMAN RACE. Dreams posses *phylogenetic* meaning, unconscious memories of the beginnings of human institutions; they represent all that is "psychologically innate in man." Thus, dreams are not to be "despised" (as Freud puts it) as sources of knowledge about the origins of humanity. They contain unconscious historical memories.

Symbolism in Cultural History

The phylogenetic elements in dreams are fossils which have survived the time when thought and speech began, and been passed from generation to generation in man's evolutionary development. The nature of ancient and primitive languages provides Freud with a strong point of comparison with his theory of dream symbols, for primitive speech reflects many of the peculiar mental qualities of dreams. (In the *General Introduction to Psychoanalysis*, Freud cites Egyptian hieroglyphics and classical Chinese as prime examples.) For instance: 1. Ancient languages are highly ambiguous and require patient interpretation; 2. Grammar and logical syntax are absent; 3. They rely exclusively on symbolism since nothing resembling an alphabet has yet appeared, and the context within which a symbol appears is essential to the meaning to be given that symbol, since symbols *NEVER MEAN* one thing and one thing only. The same holds true for dreams.

In reviewing a pamphlet entitled "The Antithetical Sense of Primal Words" (1910) and at the beginning of the second essay in his first major anthropological study *Totem and Taboo* (1913), Freud noticed the similarities which unite linguistic symbols to dream symbols as close relatives of the same psychological family. In both, symbols represent a double meaning, a dialectical opposition; they stand both for themselves AND THEIR OPPOSITES. The proper interpretation of a primitive linguistic glyph and a symbol in a dream can only be derived through interpreting the general sense of the text and the dream. ALL such primitive unconscious symbols are AMBIGUOUS. They possess two directly opposite meanings, and which sense is meant cannot be derived from the symbol, or word itself. The Polynesian word *"taboo,"* the ancient Latin *"sacer,"* the Greek *"agios,"* and the Hebrew *"kadesh,"* all mean both "holy," "consecrated," "sacred," as well as its opposite "unclean," "dangerous," "forbidden." This same ambivalence is found in dreams where typically symbols are REVERSED in their usage; for instance, a universal symbol of the male may be reversed to stand for the female in a given dream. ". . . in the manifest dream any element may also stand for its opposite." The principle of *Reversal into its Opposite* Freud found to be a major rule (unconscious, of course) in symbolic usage. Dreams then share the same dynamics as do ancient languages and represent the survival of the most archaic modes of thought in modern use.

Primary Elements of Freud's Symbolism

But *two elements are unique in Freud's theory of symbols* and these two elements distinguish it from all other psychological, semantic, and anthropological theories.

1. The true meaning of the symbols employed by the dreamer is *unconscious*. A primitive man can no more inform us of the true meaning of his tribal totem for instance, than the dreamer can tell us the meaning of the symbols he employs in dreaming. THE WHOLE TECHNIQUE OF SYMBOLIZATION has been *inherited* by mankind and its dynamics remained unconscious until Psychoanalysis discovered the essence of this archaic process.

2. By far the greater number of symbols are SEXUAL in nature.

Freud applied these two qualifications universally. *ALL* men in *all times* and *all* places symbolize in exactly the same way.

Symbolism is the same for a European city-dweller, an Australian aborigine, an Eskimo, a Polynesian, an American Indian or an ancient Egyptian. This claim has been one of the most hotly disputed in the entire theory of dreams. Freud's opponents point to the wide variations in patterns of cultural behavior to be found in the above mentioned societies. How can this Freudian claim be justified?

Now Freud did NOT claim that *the manifest form* of symbolism was universal, that all societies symbolized in exactly the same CONSCIOUS manner. (Anymore than it can be claimed that the Eskimo dreams the same kind of dreams as the Madison Avenue executive. This is absurd.) But congruent with the whole nature of dreams, Freud did assert that the *latent meaning* of culturally conditioned *manifest symbols* was identical. Let us examine this key notion in more detail.

Major Dream Symbols

Freud discovered the meaning of a great number of dream symbols. Any elongated object, a sword, knife, pistol, umbrella, walking stick, garden hose (and many more), symbolize the male genitalia. Caves, wooded areas, apertures, boxes (one is reminded of the Greek myth of Pandora's box) symbolize the female genitalia. Authority figures such as Kings and Queens and in many cases the dreamer's psychoanalyst represent parents. Large, powerful animals can symbolize either the dreamer's father, or his "bestial" instincts of which he is afraid. Water symbolizes birth, flying is symbolic of sexual intercourse, a uniform is the symbol of nakedness and bodily damage (mutilation) is symbolic of castration. Many other symbolic equations can be found in *The Interpretation of Dreams*. The point to remember is that these symbols are NOT LEARNED. We do not learn to dream as we learn to speak English or Swahili. Symbolic language is an innate, inherited, universal capacity of the human species.

But critics have raised the question how could an Australian aborigine employ the symbols of flying in a jet airplane as symbolic of sexual intercourse or fleeing from his psychoanalyst as symbolic of flight from the threatening father when both of these symbols (the jet plane and the psychoanalyst) are entirely beyond his experience and comprehension?

Superficially this criticism might seem valid. And Freud never disputed the fact that cultural differences will show up in the Manifest Dream. But while an aborigine could never symbolize sexual intercourse in the *form* of a jet airplane, nor represent his personal relationship to, and fear of, authority by dreaming of his psychoanalyst, he CAN AND DOES employ equivalent symbols derived from his own cultural experience as means of representing the *SAME UNCONSCIOUS (LATENT)* meanings, wishes and anxieties. He dreams of flying on the back of a giant bird or riding a cloud, or flying in a magic canoe across the skies (this last example is taken directly from the mythology of the Trobriand Islanders of New Guinea who believe that their culture began with the marriage of a brother and sister who fled a wicked uncle who was trying to destroy them in an airborne canoe.) He could certainly dream (and typically DOES) that he had offended the priest of his clan, the shaman, the witch-doctor, or the medicine man, all of these authority figures being equivalent in his experience (as parental, magical, threatening figures) to the psychoanalyst in the experience of a civilized European. The key point is that these divergent conscious dream (or myth) symbols represent EXACTLY THE SAME unconscious meanings.

A psychoanalytically trained anthropologist, Geza Roheim, actually undertook to study many primitive societies at first hand. He amassed a considerable amount of evidence in confirmation of Freud's views. This first hand documentation may be found in Roheim's book, *Psychoanalysis and Anthropology* (1950).

Although the use of dream (myth) symbols is universal, their conscious comprehension is not. Mankind has forgotten the true (latent) meaning of his myths and his dreams. That is why the process of dream-interpretation is such a difficult art to master and such a difficult theory to communicate and make convincing.

Individuation of Symbolism

It might be imagined that the knowledge of symbols would facilitate the business of dream-interpretation, at least by the psychoanalyst, but this is not the case. Although the essence of symbols is universal, their use by individual dreamers in individual dreams is not. We have already mentioned the principle of *Reversal into Its Opposite* as one difficulty that faces the dream interpreter. Another is more personal in nature. The simple appearance of a symbol can never reveal the constellation of complex and conflicting attitudes toward what or whom that symbol represents. All humans have gone through pretty much the same experiences. We all have had parents or parent-surrogates of one kind or another, but none of us has related to his parents in exactly the same manner. Hence, a parental figure in one dreamer's dream could never accurately represent the same wishes, anxieties or meanings as would another's. Also, the child's attitudes toward his parents are never simple. They are AMBIVALENT, that is, represent opposing and conflicting feelings, love and hate, tenderness and sadism, identification and rejection, and a host of others. Just *which one* of a number of conflicting attitudes is being expressed through a given dream symbol is a matter for investigation and interpretation.

Through the nature and use of symbols erects the first obstacle in the path of accurate dream interpretation, the Dream-Work is by no means limited to the manipulation of symbols. In fact the activity of dreaming is so complex and creative that it is worthy of being ranked with the finest products of human psychology. (Freud once called the dream an individual art work.)

Visual Form of Symbols

All dreams occur in the form of VISUAL IMAGES which must be translated into WORDS, CONCEPTS AND LOGICAL RELATIONS in order for us to understand them.

This translation of visual images into words and concepts is the very *sine qua non* of our comprehension of unconscious mental processes. For Freud, to be conscious and thus be rendered intelligible to our reason, meant *to be able to be put into words*. The meaning of dreams meant the verbal-meaning. To understand the unconscious we must be able to put it into words. Verbalization represented for Freud the highest achievement of human intelligence.

It is obvious that the translation of images into words is no small task. But even greater difficulties face the dream interpreter. For the Censor's chief method of dream distortion IS NOT the use of symbols, but a subtle process which Freud named DISPLACEMENT.

Displacement

The simplest definition of Displacement is that what occurs as material of the greatest importance in the *Latent Dream* (the Dream-Thoughts, wishes, the true purpose of the dream) appears in the Manifest Dream as trivial or meaningless. Displacement distorts and disguises what is important (but also what is forbidden access to consciousness) and makes it to appear insignificant. Displacement may be of ideas proper, but it is most often employed to shift the *affective, emotional* emphasis from the essential (in the Latent Dream) to the trivial (in the Manifest Dream). It is a most subtle and difficult process to comprehend, and the student is referred to Freud's discussion of the detailed mechanism of Displacement in the 11th chapter of the *General Introduction to Psychoanalysis*.

Condensation

In addition to the activity of Symbolization, Displacement, and the requisite translation of images into words, a further piece of Dream-Work occurs called CONDENSATION. The term means exactly what it seems to mean. A large number of unconscious Dream-Thoughts are "condensed" and appear in the Manifest Dream as one thought, or wish or person. Freud spoke of dreams (as well as all psychic acts) as *"over-determined."* By this he meant that no simple, single explanation could hope to account for the myriad thoughts, impulses, wishes, and anxieties which constituted the Manifest Dream. The Manifest Dream is ALWAYS LESS RICH IN CONTENT (i.e., MEANING) than the *Latent* Dream-Thoughts whose elements appear in an abbreviated form in the dream. Thus, a wide variety of unconscious thoughts and feelings can appear as a single element in the dream. (The opposite is NEVER the case. The Manifest Dream is always less rich in content than the Latent Dream-Thoughts). A simple example may aid us here. A king appears to us in our Manifest Dream. But a potentially unlimited number of attitudes toward authority may be "condensed" in this single manifest-dream element. (In fact, they must be, if Freud's theory of ambivalence is correct.) Hence, the single authority figure in the Manifest Dream will be a condensation of more than one unconscious attitude in the Latent Dream.

"Logic" of Dreams

We have implied that the act of dreaming represents for Freud the most primitive kind of mental functioning. Dreams are not subject to the laws of logic, consciousness and reality which govern more refined thinking. Yet Freud called the mental operations of the unconscious mind the PRIMARY PROCESS! How does the primary process differ from what we take to be the normal activity of the human mind?

As was stated earlier, Freud called the unconscious the "Kingdom of the Illogical." By this phrase he meant to illustrate just how far removed from what we take to be normal thinking-willing-feeling the Primary Process really is.

First: The Law of Contradiction which governs all conscious ratiocination (the basis of science as well as our everyday experience), DOES NOT OPERATE in the unconscious. Contradictions are held with equanimity. NOTHING IS IMPOSSIBLE TO THE DREAM!

Second: The dream cannot literally signify the conception of negation. *NO* does not exist in the unconscious.

These two "laws of the illogical" tell us why all sorts of absurdities and impossibilities occur and are accepted in dreams. Dreams are governed by the laws of wish-fulfillment, not by the laws of Aristotelian logic! And to the wish nothing is impossible!

Highly abstract logical relations such as *either/or, if/ then, because, although, just as,* as well as any concepts associated with *Time,* can only be presented *visually* in the dream, and the intended logical implications must be recognized in the process of interpretation. Even the structure of the dream can be analyzed, as a critic might analyze a play. Many short dreams, which precede the lengthier activities of a night's dreaming, function as prologues, and much of the particular dream's meaning must be guessed from its location relative to the overall dream.

And finally, an activity Freud called "secondary elaboration" occurs in which the conscious demand for intelligibility even in dreams presses forward. The dream is made "more" intelligible to consciousness, and at the same time further distorted by the activity of secondary elaboration, applying its logical demands for coherence to an activity which operates independent of these demands. The final censorship occurs in the conscious recollection of the dream, which Freud found to be unavoidably distorted. But it matters as much what we THINK we dreamed as what we actually did dream. This unfamiliar idea will be further discussed below when we encounter "Screen Memories."

Discovery of Oedipus Complex Through Dreams

By this time the beginning student will surely have raised the question, *"Why* is all the elaborate Dream-Work necessary?" Why is the whole business of disguising and distorting wishes gone through every night of an individual's life? And what is the nature of the COMPROMISE effected by the Dream-Work?

The answer was unravelled by Freud in four years of self-analysis and then re-affirmed again and again in the analysis of his patients' dreams. The unconscious wishes which generate the entire intricate, and complex activity of dream-making are not just any kind of wish. Nor, as might be reasonably anticipated, are the dream wishes simply sexual in nature. If this were so, then in an age of comparative sexual permissiveness and radically changing moral values such as our own, it might be expected that the need for dreams would severely diminish if not altogether disappear. It is necessary to recall that dreams give hallucinatory expression to INFANTILE wishes and that infantile wishes are among the most tenacious and enduring of all human wishes. At the very core of the dream-wish, Freud made his most important and enduring discovery, the existence of the *OEDIPUS COMPLEX* (named after the mythical king of ancient Greece who killed his father and married his mother), which remains today *the central doctrine of Psychoanalysis*.

A significant difficulty concerning the scientific status of Psychoanalysis first presents itself with Freud's theory of dreams. This criticism eventually extends to the whole of Psychoanalysis, so it will be well to deal with it in a general way here, and return to it specifically in the case of each particular occasion when it arose.

Many of the dreams Freud relates in *The Interpretation of Dreams* are his own. The critical implication followed that his theory grew out of his own experience, and this is not entirely incorrect. But it has been further intimated that the overweening importance Freud placed on the Oedipus Complex sprang from his own personal relationship to his father and mother and that because of this "subjective" factor, the whole of Psychoanalysis, dream-interpretation, the theory of the Oedipus Complex, the theory of neurosis, etc., cannot be extended to include all men. Cultural relativists assert that Freud's patients were, for the most part, middle-class, Jewish, Victorian Hausfraus; hence, his theories concerning the universality of repressed sexuality as the prime causal factor in the etiology of neuroses cannot legitimately be extended to other cultures and especially, to other times which differ so radically from Freud's. Freud, of course, was convinced of the scientific objectivity of his findings. The criticism that he had "projected" his own Oedipal conflicts onto his patients and by extension, to the whole human race, are irrelevant and miss the point.

Since *all men* are subject to the Oedipus Complex then of course Freud would suffer from it. But to accuse him of *subjectivity* and *projection* and *assert* that Psychoanalysis is merely the personal psychology of its founder illegitimately ascribed to the whole of humanity, is once again to ignore Freud's *evidence*, and commit the grave logical error (*argumentum ad hominem*) of arguing against the man.

Freud's Sexual Theories

1. *Studies in Hysteria* (1895)
2. *Three Essays on the Theory of Sexuality* (1905)
3. *A General Introduction to Psychoanalysis* (1915-17)
4. *An Outline of Psychoanalysis* (1939)

Although his name will forever be associated with the most revolutionary discoveries in the study of human sexual behavior, Freud did not begin his intellectual career with a specific interest in sexuality. Nor did he consider himself highly as a practitioner of medicine. His first love was the field of physiological research (in which he made a number of important findings), and had he had his wish, he would have preferred to spend his scientific life in laboratory investigations.

But, in the Vienna of the 1880's, the only field of medical practice which promised an income sufficient enough to enable him to marry and at the same time contribute to the support of his indigent family was the study of what was then termed "nervous disorders" or neuroses (from the Greek word *neuron*: nerve). Not much was known, except in a haphazard way, about the cause and cure of Hysteria (Greek, *hysteron*: womb), a somewhat vague nervous complaint from which many Viennese women suffered. A complete *symptomatology* had been described in the medical literature (that is, a listing of the kinds of behavioral abnormalities or symptoms of Hysteria), but the specific *etiology* (cause) remained a mystery. Physical disturbances including tachycardia (very rapid heart beat), fainting, exhaustion, *twilight* states of consciousness in which marked changes in normal behavior and consciousness took place, and the most debilitating symptom of all, complete paralysis of various limbs (arms, legs, hands) would occur for which *NO ORGANIC CAUSE* could be found.

Clues to Hysteria

Acting upon the advice of several senior colleagues, the young Freud went to the Sorbonne in Paris to study under the greatest psychiatrist of the day, Charcot, and it was there that he accidentally stumbled upon the first of *three major clues* which led him to the discovery of the cause of Hysteria and set him squarely on the road of sexual investigation for the remainder of his long life. In the *Autobiography* (1935), he recalled these three pivotal experiences as instrumental in directing his thinking: first, to the sexual causes of Hysteria; second, to the sexual causes of ALL NEUROSES; and finally, to the discovery of the omnipresence of sexual factors in ALL HUMAN BEHAVIOR.

It was a casual remark which the great Charcot made at a social gathering in his home that gave Freud his first insight into the sexual cause of nervous disease. Freud overheard the master in an animated discussion with a fellow physician concerning a particularly difficult hysterical woman who had been almost totally incapacitated by her

THE INTERPRETATION OF DREAMS

38   **THE INTERPRETATION OF DREAMS**

affliction. In a most emphatic manner Charcot argued that
*"Dans ces cas pareils, c'est toujours la chose genitale...
toujours... toujours!* ("In such cases, it is always a matter
of genitality, always, always!") What amazed Freud in this
declaration was the fact that Charcot had NEVER even
hinted at this etiological factor in his university lectures
which were delivered to practicing physicians!

Upon his return to Vienna, Freud received a referral from
another physician, an older colleague named Chrobak. The
patient was a woman who had suffered for years from a
severely debilitating hysteria. Chrobak wrote Freud stating
that most physicians knew the *cause and cure* for Hysteria,
but that they were unable to recommend it. He then wrote
out the prescription, *"Penis Normalis Dossim Repetitur,"* a
normal penis in repeated doses!

The final clue came to Freud in his collaboration with a
brilliant physician, Dr. Joseph Breuer, a man 14 years his
senior with whom he shared a warm personal relationship
(and who loaned Freud the money for his stay in Paris). Although he was later to retract his views and break personally with Freud, in the beginning of their collaboration
in the study of Hysteria, Breuer informed Freud that this
particular neurosis "... always hid the secrets of the marriage bed." The door had been opened and the right direction indicated, but it was Freud alone who was to tread the
lonely path, the "royal road to the unconscious."

"Studies in Hysteria" (With Breuer) (1895)

This work is justly called the first book in Psychoanalysis. It was written in collaboration with Breuer who
eventually disassociated himself from Freud's sexual theories, although, at times he seemed on the verge of "being
converted" to them (as Freud wrote), and on one note-
worthy occasion, Breuer publicly defended the sexual theory
of Hysteria before the Society of Physicians in Vienna. A
portentous sidelight to this event ocurred when Freud called

Breuer aside to thank him. He "destroyed my pleasure," Freud wrote, by saying, "All the same, I don't believe it... I can't." Although at the time Freud was completely unaware of the reasons for this peculiar behavior, he was soon to discover that this kind of reaction to his discoveries was typical among his colleagues. More will be said on this point below.

In later years Freud's attitude toward Breuer vacillated widely (perhaps an expression of the emotional *Ambivalence* which seems to have been Freud's most typical attitude). At times he would give what was perhaps more than due credit to Breuer as the discoverer of truths which became the cornerstone of Psychoanalysis. At other times, Breuer's contributions were dismissed. But in reading the *Studies in Hysteria,* one is struck by the almost total lack of specifically sexual information. Perhaps this is why Freud later was to refer to the *studies* as a "museum piece."

It is clear, however, that Breuer did contribute a number of findings (unsystematic as they were) which do play an integral part in the development of Freud's theories. Among these we may list the concepts of *CATHEXIS, ABREACTION,* and what Breuer termed *CONSCIENCE SECONDE* (secondary consciousness). The first two concepts summarize Breuer's *CATHARTIC METHOD* in the treatment of Hysteria. The third term is the precursor of the *Freudian unconscious.* These constitute a starting point a mere outline but an important one, for the Psychoanalytic theory of the relationship between *REPRESSED* sexual processes and mental illness. In his contribution to the book Freud employs for the first time the term "psychical analysis."

Freud's theory of the nature and function of human sexuality is complex, difficult and unique. His beliefs concerning the manner in which sexuality and neurosis are related underwent profound changes. And the importance of the *instinct for aggression* in the total picture of human behavior reached such a point of development, in the years 1920-1930 with the theory of the *Death Instinct,* that it nearly eclipses the sexual instincts altogether. His thinking on the nature and function of the instincts also underwent a profound alteration. Freud's theories *after* 1920 present severe modifications of all the discoveries he had made before.

Freud's Theory of Sexuality

Let us first examine the discoveries about the sexual function which are best explained in *The General Introduction to Psychoanalysis* (still the very finest introductory book on Psychoanalysis). Then, in *Section Three* of the current work (on *Metapsychology*), we shall examine those speculations which exercise an important retrospective influence on Freud's theory of human sexuality.

The following are the central ideas constituting Freud's view of sexuality:

1. From the period of his collaboration with Breuer the concepts of Cathexis, Abreation, Conversion.
2. The Oedipus Complex.
3. Infantile Sexuality (Polymorphous Perverse).
4. The Psychosexual Stages of Development. The Erotogenic (Erogenous) Zones, Oral-Anal-Phallic-Genital.
5. Fixation and Regression.
6. Repression.
7. Libido.
8. The Pleasure Principle and the Reality Principle.
9. The Nature of Instinct.
10. Anxiety.
11. Screen-Memories.

In his initial stage of development, Freud held staunchly to a conviction that he never relinquished entirely (though it was severely modified in his later years), namely, that all *psychological* phenomena would ultimately be explained in purely *physical* terms. He was scientifically committed to the physical *Principle of Constancy* which he found best described in the writings of the nineteenth-century physicist-philosopher Gustav Fechner. Stated briefly and simply, this principle maintains that all energy systems (galaxies, atoms, animals, human beings) seek to maintain *Homeostasis,* the balance between energy which accumulates within a given system, and energy which must of necessity be discharged by that system.

Hysteria and Energy Discharge

Breuer distinguished two "kinds" of energy in his analysis of hysterical behavior, *"Bound"* and *"Tonic,"* and dimly intuited that the energy maintaining hysterical symptoms (paralysis for example) was "Bound," i.e., could not be discharged along normal physiological pathways. Despite increasing evidence, Breuer refused to accept the fact that the energy "bound" in hysterical symptoms was sexual, and that neurosis was caused by the blocking of this sexual energy from its normal paths of discharge.

This was Freud's initial discovery, one which his friend had "made," but for which he refused to take the consequences. Freud's intellectual credo was always one he had learned from Charcot: To *Look* and *Look* at the facts until they *spoke* to him. Breuer was unable to "look" at the "facts" of sexuality. Freud was. And after "looking at" eighteen well-documented cases of Hysteria, the conclusion "spoke" to Freud; when sexual energy is not discharged in normal sexual activity, it becomes "bound" in neurotic symptoms and is the true cause of both the *psychological* and *physical* illness of the hysteric.

The implication which follows from this judgment of Freud's is that in order for the hysteric (and later, all neurotics) to be freed from the neurosis, a normal discharge of sexual energy is required! But at the apogee of the Victorian Era in Europe such a socially and morally revolutionary pronouncement was unthinkable. (This was undoubtedly the reason why Dr. Chrobak had asserted that physicians could not prescribe the cure for Hysteria.) To suggest either that the hysterical illness of a married woman, her inability to achieve normal sexual gratification, was the cause of that illness, or that virginal maidens were suffering from the dammed-up energy of suppressed sexual wishes, was to attack the very fabric of the social order. For, if married women could not obtain sexual satisfaction, the fault was either with their husbands (who were incompetent, or, to put it in a psychologically meaningful manner, impotent) or with their upbringing which suffocated and denied feminine sexuality. And the mere implication that virginal maidens *possessed sexual desires,* and suffered severe impairment of normal functioning because these desires were not satisfied, was to proclaim oneself a moral monster. Freud was called a lot worse by his contemporaries! This intertwining of puritanical-moralistic attitudes with the so-called medical science of the time made it impossible for Freud to obtain an impartial and unbiased hearing for his evidence.

Cathexis and Abreaction

Although Breuer had been the first to employ the terms *CATHEXIS* and *ABREACTION* he had never done so in the specific context of sexual behavior. By *Cathexis* Bruer meant a *charge of energy attached to, adhering to, associated with* an idea, impulse, wish, etc. Freud took over this term, GAVE IT ITS SPECIFICALLY SEXUAL CONNOTATION, and never abandoned it. The energy which "charged" certain ideas and impulses, was sexual. By *Abreaction* Breuer meant that this energy associated with certain ideas and impulses had to be "discharged" in order for the hysterical symptoms to disappear. Again, he veered entirely away from the notion of sexual discharge. Freud did not, and these two discoveries of Breuer (desexualized as they were) became the cornerstones of psychoanalytical therapy. They constitute Breur's *Cathartic Method* which we might describe as one-half of the goal of Psychoanalysis. The other

half Freud discovered to be the absolutely essential requirement that the patient UNDERSTAND the nature of the
process of energetic discharge. Again, Breuer intuited this
requirement, that the patient grasp the nature of *Catharsis,*
but again he was unable to tolerate the blatant sexual behavior which invariably appeared as the patient manifested
her abreactions.

Hypnosis and Free Association

The major therapeutic technique used in the Cathartic
Method was hypnosis. Physical massage, hydrotherapy and
even electrical treatments were also employed. Pressure on
the forehead of the patient often seemed to stimulate the
flow of associations. But Freud ultimately abandoned ALL
of these operations in favor of the technique of Free Association which was discussed in relation to dream-interpretation. Freud was never a good hypnotist, but he made
some important discoveries through his early experiences
with this method.

1. No matter what material the patient would recall under hypnosis, she was totally unable to recollect it in
   the waking state. While the relief of symptoms was
   achieved by hypnosis, it was short-lived and soon the
   patient would relapse into hysterical behavior.

2. The patient's sexual intentions, wishes, memories and
   fantasies while she was under hypnosis were clear to
   Freud. One of Breuer's patients (the famous Anna O.)
   actually experienced a FANTASY-PREGNANCY
   while hypnotized, and Breuer was (acclaimed) as the
   father! One of Freud's first patients embraced him
   during the therapeutic session.

3. The first faint indication given Freud of the nature
   of Free Association was when one patient he was
   questioning during therapy peremptorily told him to
   keep still and stop interrupting her flow of thoughts.

4. But undoubtedly the greatest discovery Freud made at this time came as a result of the GREATER ERROR he committed! THIS DISCOVERY WAS A TURNING POINT IN THE HISTORY OF PSYCHOANALYSIS. Freud had naively taken his patients at their word. He accepted everything as true which they reported to him in the hypnotic state. As he progressed more deeply into the *"second-consciousness"* (Breuer's term) of his patients, he was necessarily impressed by the universal reports of CHILDHOOD SEDUCTION. It seemed that each hysteric had been sexually assaulted by her father in childhood and that this assault was the genuine cause of her later neurosis. Although a convincing body of evidence was marshalled in support of the hypothesis of childhood seduction as the cause of Hysteria, the possibility slowly and painfully dawned on Freud that either most of the fathers of good Viennese families habitually seduced their infant daughters, or, the patients WERE LYING! (Although technically speaking the patients were lying, they themselves were unaware of the fact, it was an unconscious lie they were telling!) It was the realization that the latter was the case that led Freud to his discovery of SCREEN-MEMORIES and the overriding importance of FANTASY in the psychology of neurosis. The descriptions of infantile seduction were not memories at all, but fantasies which disguised the UNCONSCIOUS WISHES of the patient. The patient "wished" that such seductions had been the case in reality, and this wish was transformed into a SCREEN-MEMORY!

These events made it clear to Freud that in dealing with his patients, PSYCHIC REALITY was more important than PHYSICAL OR HISTORICAL REALITY! This meant that it really did not matter so much what a patient actually had experienced in childhood, or dreamed on a particular evening. What mattered, psychoanalytically speaking, was what anyone THOUGHT HE HAD EXPERIENCED OR

DREAMED. Thus, a SCREEN-MEMORY expresses an unconscious *wish-fulfillment* and not the description of an actual happening. It represents AN UNCONSCIOUS WISH FOR THE OCCURRENCE OF THE EVENT. This discovery was the true milestone separating Psychoanalysis from all other psychologies, the dominance of psychical reality over physical reality.

Psychoanalysis' principal task thus became the attempt to replace the screen-memories with a knowledge of the unconscious wishes that generated them. Freud wrestled long and hard with the problem of how to get the patient to recognize that what she was reporting as a memory was in reality A WISH! But he never lost sight of the fact that simply unmasking a fantasized memory as a wish was of no value in therapy unless the accompanying *affect* (the charge of energy bound to that unconscious wish) was also discharged. All his life Freud believed that this discharge of affect could be accomplished by words, that the somatic energy which had been CONVERTED INTO NEUROTIC SYMPTOMS could be liberated and discharged by getting the patient to "talk-out" the meaning of his symptoms. From beginning to end, Psychoanalysis was the therapy of talk.

Freud's Concept of Sexuality

Freud's discoveries produced two revolutionary revisions in all previous theories of human sexuality. First, Freud expanded the idea of sexuality to include non-genital-non-reproductive sex; he did not limit the concept of sexuality to genital-union and reproduction. Second, he discovered that the sexual function does not miraculously appear out of the blue at puberty but that it is present in every human being from infancy and undergoes a lengthy and complicated course of development. This is equivalent to saying that Freud discovered the existence of INFANTILE SEXUALITY.

Unhappily, Freud coined the term POLYMORPHOUS PERVERSE to describe the manifestations of infantile sexuality. This term implies moralistic condemnation which is completely foreign to Freud's intention. His intention was to distinguish the behavioral manifestations of childhood sex from its adult counterparts, but also, to reveal the connection between fixated infantile sexual attitudes and adult perversions. Etymologically, the term Polymorphous Perverse means sexual activity which is many-sided or which takes many forms (Greek, Poly: many, Morphous: formed) and which turns aside or away from (per-verse) its true goal.

Libido

In his investigations into the etiological factors of Hysteria, Freud posited the existence of a specifically sexual energy which he called *LIBIDO*. Libido, Freud describes as "analagous to hunger." At first he felt sure that it was a purely physical energy resembling the physical energy of which physicists spoke, but qualified by the fact that it manifested itself in human beings as a specifically sexual energy. And although he at one time came near to identifying this energy of the Libido with life-energy in general, his final judgment on its nature was a vehement rejection of C. G. Jung's desexualization of Libido. From beginning to end, Libido is for Freud the *specific sexual energy* identical with the *sexual instinct* in human beings.

It is the Libido which undergoes a process of historical development in each human from infancy through adolescence to adulthood in a series of "plateaus" which Freud called *PSYCHOSEXUAL STAGES OF DEVELOPMENT*. In each stage of the Libido's maturation, a particular region of the body and the principal organ of that region dominate the "kind" of sexual gratification sought by the individual. Thus, Freud expanded the notion of sexual pleasure to include the entire body and its EROTOGENIC ZONES (pleasure-giving zones), which include the mouth, the anus, the clitoris and the phallus.

But *just what happens* to the Libido as it passes through the various stages of psychosexual development led Freud to a more generalized theory of the Neuroses, and to his first clear-cut affirmation of the philosophy of *Dualism* (i.e., everything is the product of two quite different and opposing forces).

Pleasure and Reality Principles

Freud termed these two most general "principles of mental functioning" the *PLEASURE PRINCIPLE* and the *REALITY PRINCIPLE*. The term "pleasure" needs no further clarification but his use of the term Reality Principle does, for Freud does not employ the word "reality" in quite the ordinary sense. By the concept *Reality Principle* Freud means SOCIETY and the myriad demands it makes upon its members. Reality does not mean ultimate reality as it does in metaphysics or science, and it does not mean Nature. It means the demands which civilization places upon the instincts of the individual.

Originally (biologically), the Pleasure Principle rules the individual's mental life and all human behavior is motivated by the search for pleasure and the avoidance of pain. But the individual's demands for pleasure unavoidably encounter the prohibitions of society which demand conformity. Thus, the Pleasure Principle undergoes severe modification at the hands of the Reality Principle.

The world of the infant, one of boundless egoism, is totally unaware of the demands of the Reality Principle. It is ruled exclusively by the search for pleasure. But the infant quickly is made to realize that his demands cannot be met. Complete and continuous gratification are denied him and he slowly begins to develop a sense of reality and learns to modify his demands for pleasure. But the only way in which the modification of the Pleasure Principle can come about,

Freud argues, is through the exercise of threats and superior force by the representatives of the Reality Principle in the child's life, his parents. It is the parents who must frustrate the insatiable demands of infancy and inflict the first necessary traumas (Greek for wounds) on the child's psyche.

Oral Stage

The first stage of *Psychosexual Development* undergone by the *Libido* Freud called the Oral Stage. It occurs throughout the first year of life (roughly speaking) and during this phase the libido centers almost exclusively in the infant's mouth. His mouth is his greatest source of libidinal pleasure. Of course, the mouth is the vital organ of nourishment, but above and beyond this function, it is also the source of intensely pleasurable gratification. The mouth is an erotogenic zone (erogenous zone) and just the act of sucking, independent of the ingestion of nutriment, produces profound pleasure which Freud termed "sexual." This is the reason why infants suck long after their hunger has been satisfied. And the act of sucking (oral-pleasure) retains its pleasure premium throughout human life. The adult activities of smoking and kissing are survivals of the supremacy of the oral stage into maturity.

Anal Stage

The second stage of *Psychosexual* development Freud called the anal phase. In this phase the libido "moves" from its nearly exclusive concentration in the oral zone to the child's anus. Pleasure now focuses upon the excretory functions which are enjoyed for their own sake. At this point in his development the child is completely without shame in regard to his natural bodily wastes. But the demands for *cleanliness* and *control* which Freud equated with civilization's most stringent demands upon the individual require the child to relinquish anal pleasure and acquire both sphincter control and the sense of shame and disgust.

Phallic Stage

From the anal stage the libido progresses in the normal course of psychosexual development onto the *Phallic* stage. This usually occurs somewhere in the middle of the fourth year of life and at that time, what might appear to be a more clearly adult interest is taken by children in their sexual functions. But this is not the case. The Phallic stage is one of intense *narcissism, and auto-eroticism.* The love object (another person, the mother) does not really perform the function of a mature libidinal choice. Instead, the premium is placed at this stage on BEING LOVED rather than on LOVING. And the whole personality (ego) of the little child, especially the male, is centered on his genitals. It is at this stage that knowledge of sexual differentiation appears for the first time, and the gross anatomical differences between the sexes becomes the source of *intense anxiety* in the case of little boys, and of *intense envy* in the case of little girls. Also, at this time in the history of the child's psychosexual development the true OEDIPUS COMPLEX first appears. For Freud this complex ALWAYS played a more significant role in masculine psychology than it did for women. The little boy directs his sexual attentions (not just loving or affectionate attentions, but *sexual*) toward his mother and views his father as the supreme rival for his mother's love. He wishes to posses his mother sexually and destroy his father.

Female Penis Envy

It is quite a different story for the little girl. Until this time, the biological fact of sexual difference was either not known or it was ignored by both sexes. In the *New Introductory Lectures* (1932) Freud asserted that until the Phallic stage is reached, the mother is the first love (libidinal-sexual, pleasure-giving) object OF BOTH MALE AND FEMALE INFANTS and both sexes believe that the mother possesses a penis! The discovery of the truth leads to bitter disappointment for the little girl. She employs her clitoris as the major organ of sexual pleasure (in masturbation and childhood sex-games) and develops PENIS ENVY, the wish for a penis and the belief that someday her clitoris will grow into the longed-for organ. On the other hand, the little boy in discovering that some members of the human race do not possess his highly prized organ, comes to the conclusion that females were for some reason castrated, and this conclusion is the inception of CASTRATION ANXIETY, the most terrible anxiety that ever haunts the masculine, unconscious. He fears that if he does not acquiesce in parental demands, he too will be castrated. It is this threat, occurring during the full-flowering of the Oedipus Complex, that leads the little boy to renounce his mother as a sexual-love object, and suppress his hostility toward his father as a rival for his mother's love. Theoretically then, with the destruction of the Oedipus Complex, the way will be cleared for the little male child to achieve GENITAL MATURITY (after an intervening stage which Freud called the *Latency Period* in which sexuality does not come to a halt but rather, is superseded by other more important physiological and psychological requirements). This final stage Freud defined as the *Supremacy of the Genitals in the Service of Reproduction.*

The little girl passes through an analogous phase but the lack of a penis (hence, castration fears become superfluous) conditions her history in a rather different manner than that of the little boy. Needless to say, for both sexes the passage schematically described above seldom unfolds in a straight line toward sexual maturity.

Problems of Female Sexuality

On the topic of female sexuality, Freud once remarked that after 35 years dealing with the nature and problems of women he had but one question: "What do women want?" He argued that "anatomy is destiny," that is, the biologically determined differences in the anatomical structure and functions in the male and female led to the developing of radically differing psychologies as well. Freud did not "hate" women. He was not a feminist, patriarch, sexist, masculine chauvinist. (*Pace*, woman's lib.) He simply observed that men and women display remarkably different kinds of behavior and that many more women became neurotically ill than men. Part of the explanation is undoubtedly sociological. Male and female children in all civilized societies are raised according to radically differing moral codes (the old double-standard). But the major cause of the psychological differences between the sexes was anatomical (i.e., psychosexual).

A major psychoanalytic explanation of this phenomenon was suggested in the fascinating essay "The Psychology of Women" in the *New Introductory Lectures*. The task of achieving psychosexual maturity which confronts the little girl is a much more difficult one than that which the little boy faces. This task, Freud wrote, is seldom successfully concluded. A dual task confronts the little female. From the very beginning the boy child focuses his libido on a person of the OPPOSITE SEX, his mother, and his principal organ of sexual pleasure, the penis, remains the same throughout his life. But quite the opposite is true for the little girl. HER FIRST SEXUAL-LOVE OBJECT IS ALSO HER MOTHER, A PERSON OF THE *SAME SEX*, *AND*, SHE DOES *NOT* RETAIN THE SAME ORGAN AS HER MAJOR SOURCE OF PLEASURE IN ADULTHOOD AS SHE DID IN INFANCY! The female must change BOTH the sex of her love-object choice AND the principal organ of sexual satisfaction! This is another contributing factor which differentiates the female from the male Oedipus Complex.

Theoretically, in the normal course of her psychosexual maturation, the *clitoris* LOSES its status as the primary organ of sexual pleasure and is replaced by the *vagina*. But this dual task, changing the sex of her object-choice and changing her principal sexual organ is rarely attained and most women, even those who are not neurotically disturbed, remain fixated at an infantile level of psychosexual development. Add to these uniquely feminine difficulties the fact that a woman must resolve her Oedipus Complex in relation to her father, and then be subject to the severe sexual prohibitions that civilizations inflict upon their females, and it is no wonder that so few women ever "survive" the ordeal of psychosexual development.

In qualifying Freud's theory of sexual differentiation, it must be stated that he adhered to a belief in the CONSTITUTIONAL BI-SEXUALITY of human beings and often discussed the difficulties in trying to sharply demarcate the lines which divide the male from the female.

There exist feminine "sexual" components and attitudes in all men, and vice versa. Freud analyzed one such attitude which he personally embodied, an intellectual passivity and dependence in relation to forceful, masculine friends. But he never was able to come to a final and satisfying conclusion to the most perplexing question: what is the essence of sexual differentiation? (He even once wrote in a letter that homosexuality was not to be considered an illness!)

Repression, Resistance, Fixation and Regression

It was these discoveries which constituted Freud's theory that human sexuality had a history that could be traced through definite stages, and that there exists a definite relationship between the experiences of an individual at a given psychosexual stage, and his adult neurotic behavior. Three new principles of psychoanalytic theory and therapy emerged from these discoveries, the principles of REPRESSION, RESISTANCE, and FIXATION AND REGRESSION. These comprise the core of Psychoanalysis.

Repression

Freud termed REPRESSION "... the foundation stone on which the structure of psychoanalysis rests." We have already met this crucial psychic activity in our discussion of the Censorship in the theory of dreams. It is the Censorship that carries out the Repression of forbidden wishes. But the dream-censor is but one agency among many which manifest the nature of Repression.

A preliminary linguistic distinction is necessary if we are to grasp the true nature of Repression. REPRESSION must be sharply distinguished from SUPPRESSION, and it must be stated that Freud (or his translators) do not always make that necessary distinction. In its first formulation REPRESSION IS AN UNCONSCIOUS MENTAL ACTIVITY WHICH SEEKS TO SEPARATE CONSCIOUSNESS FROM THE UNCONSCIOUS. The absolutely essential point to note is that REPRESSION IS ENTIRELY UNCONSCIOUS in its activity. The individual does not know that he is repressing certain forbidden material. On the other hand, SUPPRESSION is a *conscious* and *deliberate* act. An impulse to strike my superior or make an off-color remark to a woman may appear in my consciousness. I then *suppress* that impulse. But if my psyche contains unconscious wishes concerning my attitude toward my superior or women which I cannot consciously accept, I shall then *repress* them, deny that they exist, and perhaps produce some compromise formation which will allow the unconscious wish access to consciousness in a disguised and distorted form.

It is the Repression of sexual impulses that is the cause of the formation of neurotic symptoms. Instead of finding its way into the outer world, the impulse is blocked and deflected into a symptom which is another instance of a compromise formation. The symptom is a substitute for sexual gratification brought about by the Repression of an impulse.

Resistance

RESISTANCE and Repression go hand in hand in maintaining the mental equilibrium, the psychic status quo. The

Resistances serve as defenses against unconscious material being made conscious; that is, they are in the service of the repressions. Patients develop a whole battery of resistances in defense of their repressions. They may violate the Analytic Compact and critically reject material which presents itself to them rather than tell the analyst of it and follow the chain of free associations. They may wander from the topic, seeking intellectual enlightenment, produce no associations whatsoever or, they may even fall in love with the analyst (this form of Resistance Freud wrote was employed with a positive genius by his female patients). They may even finally reject the whole of Psychoanalysis and break off therapy. These forms of behavior are all examples of Resistance-defense in the service of the Repressions. The patient achieves what Freud called a "secondary gain" from his illness, and this is often so valuable a part of the individual's psychic equipment that he refuses to part with it even at the expense of remaining neurotic.

After all, the neurotic symptoms assist the patient in maintaining his psychological equilibrium by preventing painful and distressing thoughts and wishes from coming to consciousness. That is why he so mightily defends his neurosis through the employment of Resistances. A part of the patient's personality wants to get well but another part wishes to defend itself against the anxieties and threatening impulses which must be made conscious if he is to get well. This second, repressed part of the personality wishes to remain ill. The patient is spared the painful emotional process of dissolving the resistances and lifting the repressions which is the heart of psychoanalytic therapy at the expense of getting well.

Regression and Fixation

The third R of Psychoanalysis is REGRESSION (closely bound up with the notion of FIXATION of an impulse at a pre-genital stage of psychosexual development). In the neurotic the libido tends to regress to earlier stages of psycho-sexual organization when it finds itself severely frustrated in reality. When the progress of the libido is impeded and stops short of its goal of the Genital Stage, it returns to the last stage of psychosexual development reached BEFORE the traumatic frustration occurred and remains fixated at that level. The Regression of the libido to pre-genital modes of functioning and its fixation at these levels account for the variety of behavioral aberrations in the adult which are termed neuroses or perversions.

Let us examine these principles in more detail. Freud argued that human behavior represents a compromise be-tween the two principles of mental functioning, the Pleas-ure Principle, and the Reality Principle. The dominance of the Pleasure Principle in psychic life is slowly replaced by the Reality Principle which the child encounters in the demands for instinctual renunciation made upon him by his parents. These demands are accompanied by threats either open or implied but they are always interpreted by the child as meaning the loss of the parent's love and more specifically, in the case of the little boy, the loss of his penis through castration. Adhering to Fechner's Principle of the Constancy of Energy in any given system (home-ostasis), Freud argued that the energy of the libido must "go somewhere" when it is blocked from discharge. Some of this energy receives gratification in a disguised form in dreaming. But in the neurotic, most libidinal energy is repressed and converted into symptoms. The term Cathexis (charge of energy associated with an idea, impulse or wish) gave rise to its dialectical opposite COUNTER-CATHEXIS. By Counter-Cathexis Freud meant the charge of energy as-sociated with the forces of REPRESSION which are directed against the unconsciously cathected ideas, wishes and im-pulses and which prevent them access to consciousness or gratification. Most of the neurotic's libido then is bound up in the Counter-Cathexis of the Repressions and in symptoms.

The Neuroses

Orality

The fixation of the libido at pre-genital levels gives rise to adult neuroses, perversions, and strongly exaggerated forms of what we call normal behavior. If an infant passed through an entirely unsatisfactory oral stage or a traumatic one, much of his libido would remain fixated at this earliest stage of libidinal organization. A mother might frustrate the infant's intense desire to suck for pleasure and though no conscious memory of this traumatic event would remain, and given certain other developmental factors, this infant might well mature into an adult with an oral-fixation. His adult behavior would be in large measure the result of his infantile oral frustrations. His mouth would remain an overly-cathected erogenous zone, and many of his adult behavioral patterns would manifest themselves as a search for oral pleasure. He might become a heavy smoker (Freud himself smoked twenty cigars a day), or if he had reached the second half of the oral stage, the oral-aggressive stage at which infants manifest aggression through biting, and had been frustrated there, he might develop into an adult who used his mouth to say "biting" things about others, a lawyer, a critic, or a politician.

Anality

Certain adult character traits, both normal and neurotic, are results of a traumatic anal-phase of psychosexual development. In fact, Freud explained the genesis of the Obsessive-Compulsive neurosis by tracing its behavioral peculiarities to traumatic toilet training. The obsessive-compulsive neurotic is characterized by an overwhelming need for cleanliness. The woman who compulsively cleans all the ash trays in her house as soon as they have been used, or the man who showers six or seven times a day in the name of "cleanliness" are examples. This conscious absorption with being clean is actually a REACTION FORMATION;

that is, a defense against the forbidden wish to do just the opposite, be filthy. A traumatically sanitary mother forces the infant into cleanliness long before he is willing or able to control his excremental functions, and produces the fixation at the anal level which is one of the most difficult of all therapeutic problems. The principal character traits of this type of adult are doubt, indecision and distrust. He is also usually very stubborn.

The compulsive character is also typified by the compelling need to carry out certain ritualistic performances in a rigidly predetermined manner, and if prevented from doing so, is overwhelmed by the most intolerable anxiety. His behavior acts again as a defense against unconscious wishes and impulses which produced threatening situations in childhood.

Phallic Genitality

Perhaps the two most common neurotic types met in daily life are the Hysteric and the Phallic-Narcissist; indeed their behavioral patterns are generally equated with normalcy. The sexual attitude and behavior of the contemporary Hysteric bear no apparent resemblance to the neurotic symptoms of the Hysterics of Freud's time. But the difference is superficial and does not affect the deep-lying unconscious mechanisms which are the same. The Hysteric cannot tolerate her own sexual feelings but, paradoxically, she defends herself against anxiety-producing unconscious oedipal impulses, by EMPLOYING SEXUAL BEHAVIOR AS A DEFENSE AGAINST SEXUALITY. Though this type is often quite attractive and sexually provocative in her attitudes and actions, she is actually running from deep sexual feelings through casual liaisons with men for whom she does not feel deeply and who do not arouse the anxieties associated with her sexual advances toward her father in childhood, her first love object, advances which were severely rebuffed, usually by a highly moralistic mother. While physical disabilities do not play as large a part in the overt symptoms of the contemporary Hysteric as they did in the nineteenth century, still, much of the Hysteric's libido is blocked from normal discharge and she suffers the vague complaints which we have come to call psychosomatic. In therapy, the Hysteric, above all other types, "runs away" from therapy by falling in love with the analyst. As will be discussed below, this falling in love is simply another Resistance against getting well.

The Phallic-Narcissist male also employs a hyperactive sexuality as a defense against profound unconscious castration anxiety. He is the Don Juan, Cassanova type. But his need to conquer every woman he meets is the result of a deep unconscious fear of homosexuality. He must constantly prove himself a man. At the Phallic stage in his development, his sexual exhibitionism was met with severe reproofs or punishment and in order to preserve his penis from the imaginary castration threats, the boy unconsciously adopts a passive-feminine role in relation to his father, and renounces his mother as a sex-object. In adulthood, he is unable to love maturely; that is, to accomplish what Freud called the most difficult task in the life of a man, to unite the streams of tenderness and sensuality which he originally felt toward his mother in a relationship with a mature woman. He runs from this relationship because it evokes unconscious threats of punishment, just as his first love toward his mother evoked real ones. Hence, his attitude toward women is contemptuous and he can never allow feelings of tenderness to emerge. He unconsciously equates his phallus with a weapon with which he punishes women. But like the Hysteric he is compelled to flee anxiety-provoking sexual feelings through indiscriminate promiscuity.

The Perversions

Freud defined neurosis as "the negative of the perversions," meaning by this that the neurotic repressed his forbidden sexual impulses, while the pervert acted them out.

He was one of the first to approach sexual perversions from a medical-scientific perspective, rather than a moralistic-condemnatory one, and he presents us with the first genuine scientific understanding of their nature.

The sexual pervert is strongly fixated at a given level of infantile development but, unlike the neurotic who produces symptoms as resolutions of his conflicts, he engages in deviant behavior. Adult perversions are to be explained in terms of Freud's theory of psychosexual development. PERVERSIONS ARE SIMPLY THE INFANTILE SEX LIFE CARRIED ON INTO ADULTHOOD.

Pre-Genitality

What can be termed "normal" at a given stage of the infantile sexual development, i.e., exhibitionism, masturbation, voyeurism, homosexual play, become "abnormal" when in adulthood THEY REPLACE THE FINAL AIM AND PURPOSE OF MATURE SEXUALITY: HETEROSEXUAL, GENITAL UNION. The pre-genital libido is diffuse in its objects, seeking only bodily pleasure. It has not yet become organized and directed toward its natural goal. For Freud, nothing is "perverse" in an impulse per se. An impulse becomes perverted only when pre-genital modes of sexual gratification REPLACE heterosexual genital union AND BECOME EXCLUSIVE. It was the exclusivity of any pre-genital impulse usurping the natural goal of genitality that defined it as perverse for Freud.

But any pre-genital impulse brought into the service of heterosexual union cannot be considered perverse. Freud's thinking was fluid, tolerant, and reserved in judgment in matters concerning what we term normal sexuality in relation to what we term the "abnormal." If by normal sexuality we mean the "norm," that is, the sexual practices of most not-grossly disturbed adults or the prescribed sexual mores of a given civilization, then by normal we could not mean the ideal, the best, or the healthiest. Freud strenuously rejected the unrealistic sexual attitudes of most civilized communities. One of the major goals of psychoanalytic therapy is the alleviation of the enormous guilt-feelings about sex which society inculcates in its members. And paradoxically, much deviant behavior is a search for punishment caused by the powerful unconscious feelings of guilt.

Certainly homosexuality is to be classified abnormal since it blocks access to the natural goal of heterosexual genital union. It represents a severe fixation at the Phallic level. It presents us with what Freud called "a stage of arrested development." Yet his lifelong conviction of the bisexual constitution of human beings prevented Freud from viewing homosexuality strictly in terms of illness.

Yet, even the most wildly deviant sexual behavior is simply the *exaggeration* of one or more components of normal sexuality. Perversions are hyper-exaggerations of normality. One guiding principle of psychoanalytic theory is what we may call the Principle of Psychological Continuity. All mental events are related. There exist no sharp, qualitative "breaks" in mental functioning. The abnormal is an exaggeration of the normal. Any pre-genital impulse which submits to the PRIMACY OF THE GENITALS IN THE SERVICE OF REPRODUCTION cannot be called perverse.

The Goals and Obstacles of Psychoanalytic Therapy

Freud was keenly aware that the therapeutic goal of Psychoanalysis must of necessity include some criteria of "normalcy" or "cure." If the psychoanalytic theory of neurosis and perversion was correct, then what criterion could be established to determine the successful termination of therapy? When and how had a patient's behavior changed sufficiently to allow the analyst to dismiss him as "cured," or at least less neurotic or perverse than before entering therapy?

Let us undertake a brief résumé of the material dealt with before pursuing this question further. Freud believed Psychoanalysis to be a medical science. He had discovered a set of definite principles of mental functioning, their relationship to mental illness, and a method for converting sickness back into health. This method included Free Association and the Interpretation of Dreams as its major techniques. Health could be restored by getting the patient to recollect and talk about traumatic experiences from his childhood. Bound libido was released when resistances were dissolved, repressions lifted and symptomatic behavior replaced by normal behavior. A major theoretical and practical difficulty appears at this point in the development of Psychoanalysis whose basic clinical discoveries have been discussed above. What is the fate of the libidinal energy when it is released from repression and symptom-formation, what happens to it, where does it go? Of perhaps all the problematic areas of Psychoanalysis this is the most crucial and on this issue Freud was most indecisive.

If illness is caused by the blockage (repression-symptom-formation) of sexual energy, then it would seem that health could only be re-established when — in addition to dissolution of resistances and lifting of repressions — the libido, once bound up in these neurotic activities, is released to achieve a satisfactory sex life. But this would made psychoanalytic therapy into an instrument of social criticism and what is more important, an *instrument of social reform*, and this Freud emphatically did NOT wish to happen. Freud refused to accept the revolutionary social implications of his greatest discoveries.

Neuroses and Civilization

And yet, if as he clearly demonstrated, repressive civilization, the oedipal family and a generally sex-negative human attitude are the principal causative agents in mental illness, it would follow that mental health requires a severe modification of these agencies. This would precipitate a struggle between the liberating forces of Psychoanalysis and the repressive forces of a sex-negative society, and Freud was never able to take that step. Repeatedly, Freud argued that civilization made individuals fall ill from the privation of natural sexual gratification, that cultural mores are entirely unrealistic in their demands for the renunciation of sexual fulfillment, that children are, for the most part, treated brutally in their sexual education with no concern for their future health or happiness, and that the moral institutions of civilization are not concerned with the individual's happiness but with his obedience and conformity. But nowhere in his writings will you find a program for the prophylaxis of neurosis before it begins. The purpose of psychoanalytic therapy is aborted before reaching its goal!

Freud was pessimistic about the treatment of neurosis once it had taken root in the personality. The sympathetic student of Freud intuits almost a sense of relief in the last twenty years of his life as his curiosity took him further and further from the problems of individual therapy into the wider problems of Metapsychology. In the beginning Freud thought that therapy need not last more than, on the average, three months. This modest estimate he then expanded to one year. Then, even greater periods of time were seen to be required for a successful outcome to therapy until finally, Freud was led to write an article entitled "Analysis Terminable and Interminable" in which he abandoned all attempts at setting time limits in therapy, but at the same time warned analysts that analysis might conceivably replace the patient's neurosis in his psychic economy (he would develop "an analytic neurosis") at which time, the knowledgeable analyst would set the time limit or break off therapy.

Further difficulties began to appear with the discoveries of RESISTANCE (which has been thoroughly discussed above) and TRANSFERENCE. The unconscious exploitation of the Transference relationship which develops in every analysis becomes one of the major weapons employed by the Resistances and a major obstacle to successful therapy.

Transference

By the Analytic Transference Freud meant the following: the patient gradually "transfers" unconscious attitudes which he once experienced in relation to his parents, to the person of the analyst, who thus becomes a substitute-parent. The patient then unconsciously relives his infantile sexual wishes and fantasies in therapy with his physician. But he also unconsciously employs this tender erotic attitude as a defense against becoming aware of repressed impulses. Hence, transference love acts as a resistance against getting well.

Freud ironically remarked that a number of his female patients had evinced an obvious sexual interest in him which he could not account for by his own irresistible masculine charm. This modesty enabled him to discover the true nature of the transference. Now while the transferences do function as resistance, they can also function as allies of the analyst and that part of the patient's psyche which wishes to get well. The POSITIVE TRANSFERENCE (falling in love with the analyst as a symbolic father or mother) makes the patient wish to please the analyst and often a definite remission of neurotic symptoms appears. But the analyst must both understand and reject the erotic overtures which become more and more insistent as treatment progresses. It was not HE, SIGMUND FREUD who was being "loved" by his patients, but rather HE AS A SURROGATE FATHER.

Negative Transference

The analyst must handle the transferences with the utmost delicacy and seek to point out to the patient how he or she is exploiting them as defenses against repressed impulses. The stage of the POSITIVE TRANSFERENCE invariably leads to the stage of the NEGATIVE TRANS-FERENCE, which Freud always took to be the MOST

DIFFICULT PROBLEM IN THERAPY which if mis-
handled could wreck the most promising therapeutic relationships. As the patient's overtures (sometimes crassly
sexual) are rejected by the analyst, a situation similar to
that in childhood occurs. The patient's thwarted infantile
love turns to hatred as he unconsciously relives through the
analyst the whole of his relationship with his parents. During the stage of the NEGATIVE TRANSFERENCE the
patient often relapses into the worst kind of neurotic behavior and relinquishes whatever gains he may have made
to that point in therapy. He becomes disparaging of the
analyst and of analysis in general, complains that it has
done him no good or made him worse than ever, disparages
the person of the analyst, misses appointments for his
therapeutic hour, threatens to break off analysis, and often
does so.

If the patient can be made slowly aware of the true nature of the transference processes and how he employs
them as resistances, then therapy can usally give a happy
prognosis. If not, it is impossible for therapeutic progress
to continue and the analysis had best be terminated.

Counter-Transference

But the transference situation is further complicated by
the fact that the analyst too is involved as a human being
with his own unconscious impulses, complexes, anxieties
and needs. This fact was brought home most cogently to
Freud by the practice of the Hungarian psychoanalyst,
Sandor Ferenczi, undoubtedly Freud's "favorite son" among
all his pupils. Ferenczi would respond to his patient's overtures, quite aware of what he was doing, by literally "baby-
ing" them, deliberately playing the surrogate-parent role
and claiming great therapeutic success. Freud was initially
open to this novel approach. But when the whole nature of
the transference situation became apparent, with the discovery of the COUNTER-TRANSFERENCE, he then re-

jected it. It was found that analysts would often unconsciously respond themselves to their patients' unconscious
allurements and provocations. They would respond to both
the positive and negative reactions of their patients, OUT
OF THEIR OWN PERSONAL UNCONSCIOUS NEEDS.
When this happens, the analytic situation is destroyed. Unless an analyst can recognize and rationally handle his
own counter-transferences, he is worse than useless as
a therapist.

If the complex and difficult problems presented above
can be resolved what then is the purpose of Psychoanalysis
to be? Freud vacillated between restrained optimism (he always referred to himself a "cheerful pessimist") and cold
intellectual pessimism, finally asserting that the real value
of Psychoanalysis lay in its capacity for explaining the nature and origin of cultural institutions rather than its
ability to alleviate mental suffering. Yet, he never fully
abandoned the conviction that Psychoanalysis was the finest
technique available for handling the neuroses.

In the *Introductory Lectures* Freud describes Psychoanalysis as a species of RE-EDUCATION which assists the
patient in recollecting the repressed and forgotten memories which made him fall ill, and by so doing, allow him to
"become the kind of individual he would have become had
not the neurosis interrupted his development toward maturity." Psychoanalysis is unable to take sides with the
totally unpsychological demands made by culture upon the
instinctual life of the individual, but on the other hand it
cannot advise the patient to "live freely according to his
instincts, that is at least as far from our purpose as the
former." The ideal of therapy is to replace unconscious
repression of impulses, wishes and attitudes with rational
judgment, to give the patient the opportunity to make conscious decisions about his conflicts. (An interesting contradiction of Freud's complete denial of freedom of the will.)
The goal may thus be summarily stated as "making the unconscious conscious."

Sublimation

Freud was never an exponent of instinctual gratification as the guide to life; in fact, he seems to have heartily disliked man's instinctual makeup. His aim was intellectual control of the instincts. But a subtle and profound change thus occurs in the psychoanalytic philosopy of life. In place of the active search for happiness which is the program of the Pleasure Principle and which can only be reached through instinctual gratification, Freud advocates the *renunciation* of the instincts and the control of life through intelligence. But again Freud is caught in the dilemma of what we are to do with the imperative drives which constitute our instinctual life once they have been freed from repressions. His answer is SUBLIMATION.

The concept of Sublimation plays an increasingly important role in the development of Freud's cultural theories and is one of civilized man's major accomplishments. Sublimation is the psychic activity which REDIRECTS the energy of the libido from sexual outlets into higher and more valuable social and cultural activities. Freud discovered the philosopher Plato's description of the process in complete agreement with his own, though Plato did not use the term. The process of desexualizing libidinal energy, inhibiting its aim and changing its direction is the source of all creative activity by civilized man. Artists are especially gifted with this capacity as are intellectual workers. But ordinary mortals must employ Sublimation too in dealing with their instincts, though they are much less gifted than artists and thinkers. Sublimation produces secondary-gratifications of the instincts which, because of the repressive nature of civilization, cannot find direct satisfaction. It represents man's most highly developed and distinct psychological capacity.

"The Psychopathology of Everyday Life" (1907)

We have discussed in detail Freud's theories of mental pathology. But Psychoanalysis as the most complete and definitive psychology of human behavior seeks to explain the normal as well and link it in some way to the same dynamics that determine abnormal mental activity. Freud sought to show the connections between the unconscious and normal, everyday occurrences in his little book *The Psychopathology of Everyday Life* (1907). Again, this title is somewhat misleading as was Freud's usage of the term Polymorphous Perverse. By Psychopathology Freud did not mean that everyone is "crazy" in his day-by-day occupations (although he did assert in a later work that the whole human race suffered from neurosis in greater or lesser degree). He meant simply to show that psychic conditions, which when exaggerated or traumatized lead to neurosis, can also be found in normal mental functioning, another example of what we termed Freud's Principle of the Unity of Mental Functioning.

The fact of psychological determinism is strongly affirmed once again, though now in the realm of the normal. For Freud, there exist no "accidents" in the mental life, normal or abnormal. Every manifestation of human behavior, no matter how trivial or seemingly meaningless has an explanation and a determining cause which makes it to be just that particular event and nothing else. (The Rationalist philosophers of the seventeenth century spoke of the *Principle of Sufficient Reason:* For every event there exists a determining cause, for every idea a *necessary* explanation. This is also Freud's scientific credo.)

Freud did not mean to assert that accidents per se do not exist in nature. If I am flying in an airplane which hits the side of a mountain during a rainstorm that is most emphatically an accidental death. But mental accidents do not exist, every seemingly accidental event has a cause and a reason.

It is the trivial, daily experiences with which we are all so familiar and which we casually dismiss as accidental or meaningless that Freud used to uncover the connections between the normal and abnormal and discover their common ground in the dynamics of the unconscious. Forgetting something we "ought to" remember, slight errors such as slips of the tongue, mis-spelling, mis-pronouncing, mis-reading, mis-hearing and all similar "parapraxes" express unconscious impulses, possess meaning, and as we know by now, if they are genuinely subject to the laws of unconscious mental activity, represent compromises between unacceptable or forbidden wishes and the repressing forces of consciousness.

Dreams are compromise formations. Neurotic symptoms are also. And so are all of the trivial symptomatic errors we daily commit. The compromise occurs for the dual purpose of discharging an urgent unconscious impulse which cannot be otherwise manifested, and at the same time, of maintaining the structure of conscious personality intact and defending it against disturbing intrusions from the unconscious.

Meaning of Errors

All errors are then purposeful. Forgetting, for example, especially the names of loved ones and important events in the past expresses an unconscious wish on the part of the forgetter which he cannot consciously accept. Freud relates the tale of a newly married lady of his acquaintance who saw a familiar man in the street and turned to her friend to remark, "I know that man from somewhere." She had in fact just recently married him. Freud remarked that this slip was certainly an ill-omened message from the lady's unconscious. (The marriage ended shortly thereafter.) She had expressed an unconscious wish, in forgetting her husband's identity, that he really was not her husband. When we mis-read a word that completely alters the meaning of a written passage it is because we find the intended meaning not to our liking and so we unconsciously alter it to suit our own unconscious wishes. If we mis-hear a remark addressed to us or if we ourselves utter something which we did not consciously intend to say (and as Freud points, the perpetrator of such symptomatic acts is usually totally unaware of having committed them) it is because an unconscious impulse slipped into consciousness undetected and fulfilled the wish to hear what we wanted to hear, rather than what was actually said, or uttered what we unconsciously wished to say, instead of the consciously intended remark. Losing a "treasured" or "highly prized" gift or object often (though not invariably) is the expression of an unconscious disdain for the giver, but it may also mean the desire to return to a place or situation in which the object was lost or left behind. Sometimes the loss of a really valued object operates in the form of apotropaic magic, that is, we surrender something of value in order to forestall the loss of something much more valuable or avert an unconsciously intuited calamity. And habitually calling an acquaintance or loved one by someone else's name signifies the unconscious wish that the identities be reversed.

The theories and discoveries studied in the first section of this book represent Freud's great *Clinical Period.* In the following section we will see how Freud's interests widened to include not only the problems of individual patients, but the problems of culture and civilization. In this *Cultural Period,* Freud applied the clinical techniques and discoveries made in psychoanalytic therapy to questions concerning the nature, origin and value of mankind's most precious institutions.

PART TWO

FREUD'S CULTURAL PERIOD

1. *Totem and Taboo* (1913)
2. *Group Psychology and the Analysis of the Ego* (1921)
3. *Moses and Monotheism* (1938-9)

"Totem and Taboo" (1913)

Concerning the relationship between *Totem and Taboo*, his first major study of the genesis of culture, and his previous clinical discoveries, Freud wrote that a decade earlier he had uncovered the "wish" to kill the father (in *The Interpretation of Dreams*), and now in this work, he had uncovered the "deed." Critics have inaccurately suggested that the PRIMAL HORDE theory, the kernel of this book, is simply a symbolic myth, fabricated in the manner of a dream, symbolically but not literally true. From this assertion the illegitimate inference has been drawn that Freud was merely spinning out a fantasy and giving rein to his long controlled speculative impulses. From Freud's point of view this is emphatically NOT the case with *Totem and Taboo,* which he always considered one of his major contributions to human knowledge, and it is beyond question that the events described here, he took to be historically accurate and literally true. The last words of *Totem and Taboo* are, "In the beginning was the Deed." However, some small merit may be attached to the opinion that the Primal Horde theory functions in the manner of a mythology, a piece of historical "dream-work," but only in so far as Freud argues that he has compressed into ONE single event, a whole series of pre-historic experiences which spanned generations and was repeated again and again in the infancy of the human race. But that these events did actually happen is beyond the shadow of a doubt Freud's belief, one to which he was to return years later when he wrote *Moses and Monotheism*.

A second criticism levelled at the Totem thesis by professional anthropologists was that Freud had never done any field work among primitives and lacking first-hand observations he was incompetent to judge the meaning of taboos, rituals and customs. In response to this objection we may point out that the bibliography of *Totem and Taboo* lists some 80 different authors as the sources of reference from which Freud gathered the factual material for his essays. Some of the greatest names in classical anthropology appear on this list, social scientists who *did* first hand field work in primitive communities. But it is necessary to remember that Freud's examination of the primitive mind was from the novel perspective of Psychoanalysis which was entirely foreign to the techniques of anthropology; hence, in order to pass judgment on these theories the critic would have to be versed in psychoanalytic knowledge of the unconscious. Most of Freud's anthropological critics lacked this knowledge. Consequently, they argued from a point of view which was their own, not Freud's.

The subtitle given to this work was "Some Points of Agreement between the mental lives of savages and Neurotics," and Freud made it quite clear that his ideas would appear bizarre to anyone not acquainted in some detail with the theory of Psychoanalysis. Hence, his Cultural Theory most definitely evolves from his Clinical practice.

Taboo is perhaps the more familiar of the two terms. Any person, object or activity which is taboo is strictly prohibited, forbidden, not allowed. When any event is taboo, it cannot be done, no questions asked. Taboos go beyond rational question or criticism. They are categorical prohibitions.

Totemic Origins

Totem refers to widespread pre-religious practices among primitives. Totemism includes a definitely structured social and moral order based upon the asserted affiliation with a common ancestor which is usually an animal, and membership in a Totem group rigidly prescribes all of the major events in an individual's life, especially MARRIAGE AND SEXUAL RELATIONS. Totem and taboo are thus closely wedded concepts. Totemism (the common ancestry of a given social order) defines the nature and function of taboos (the permissible sexual relations within that Totem group).

Totemic religious practices were the forerunners of the more sophisticated and humanistic religions, especially Judaism and Christianity, and seem to bear little resemblance to them, but Freud indicated that quite the opposite, was the case. One of the prime tasks of the psychoanalytic theory of culture was to demonstrate the CONTINUITY of human mentality from the primitive to the civilized and to show in what manner the power and influence of civilized institutions such as religion, morality, and the family structure, DERIVED FROM the same unconscious grounds as their more primitive precursors.

To sum up the twelve articles of Totemism which Freud used as the factual basis for his psychoanalytic interpretation, we may briefly state that members of a given Totem clan claim descent from the same common ancestor, an animal, that all of the social and moral arrangements of primitive life gravitate around this nucleus of a common descent, that it is forbidden (taboo) to kill the totem animal who exercises a magical and beneficent influence on the destiny of his totem, that INCEST with clan members (and Incest is not defined by degrees of consanguinity but by membership in the Totem clan) is the most strictly enforced prohibition and the most severely punished behavior when detected, equaling in severity the punishment meted out to clan members who kill (even inadvertently) the clan animal.

But on festival occasions the totem animal is ceremoniously killed and eaten by all the members of the clan (and participation by ALL clan members is mandatory) and, at that time, all the previously rigidly enforced taboos are lifted and indiscriminate sexual activity INCLUDING INCEST AS DEFINED BY CLAN MEMBERSHIP, is not only permitted, it is required. No member of the clan may stand aside from the totem feast and the ensuing promiscuity. From this bizarre and contradictory quality of primitive human behavior, Freud arrived at his theories of the beginnings of the institutions of civilization.

We may now further explicate the nature of Compromise Formations in mental life by describing them as the effects of unconscious AMBIVALENCE. As we have said, Freud was an inveterate dualist, that is, he was never willing or able to reduce human psychology to one single, simple set of determining attitudes. The unconscious is the realm of mental functioning wherein the Principle of Contradiction simply does not exist. Absolute opposites function side by side in the unconscious, whereas in logical terms we would speak of contradiction. In the language of the unconscious we would speak of Ambivalence, the holding of totally opposed attitudes (love and hate, reverence and irreverence, attraction and disgust, etc.) in relation to the SAME person or activity. Quite obviously the primitive's attitude toward his Totem animal and the Taboos which surround it is Ambivalent: he both protects and kills the totem animal, he both punishes and practices incest. This fundamental dialectic of Ambivalence is found in civilized men as well, and especially in the little boy's relation to his father, whom he both loves as a figure of power and punishment, and hates as a rival (Oedipus Complex) for his mother's love. This most basic psychological attitude is evinced in all humanity's (primitive as well as civilized) unconscious mind. Increasingly as time went by, Freud denied the possibility of any manifestation of the unconscious in human behavior, personal as well as social, which was simple, direct, and meant what it seemed to mean. Man is not only the animal whose behavior is the product of psychological conflicts, he is the animal whose behavior is the product of psychological *Ambivalence*. EVERY HUMAN EMOTION (with the possible exception of a mother's love for her infant child) IS AMBIVALENT!

Totem as Father Symbol

The nature of the totem animal was revealed to Freud through his study of dream symbols and phobias in children. Typically, animals symbolize the dreamer's FATHER, and the fear of animals in children is actually a transference of their fear of their father to a suitable animal surrogate. From this well-documented fact, Freud deduced that the totem animal, the animal ancestor of the clan, was quite literally the FATHER OF THE CLAN, THE HUMAN FATHER! Every individual's unconscious Ambivalence (love and hate) directed toward his father is discovered to operate as the basic mechanism explaining the clan member's ambivalent action toward his totem-animal-father (loving and protecting him for most of the year, killing and eating him at the totem festival). But what is the connection between ritual, totemic, symbolic father-murder and the lifting of the incest taboo?

Taboo

Before attempting to answer this question, Freud further examined the essence of a taboo. Taboos would be unnecessary in the case of actions or thoughts which an individual does NOT wish to carry out. It is not necessary to place a taboo upon sticking one's hand into a fire. The essential nature of any taboo is that it is levelled against actions and thoughts which human beings, civilized as well as primitive, most ardently desire to perform (though the wish to carry out the tabooed action is unconscious). This is one of the major reasons why taboos are not to be questioned but unthinkingly obeyed. The questioning of a taboo (against Incest for example, the most universally tabooed of all human actions) would provoke intolerable anxiety and it is just this unconscious anxiety connected to the forbidden wish that the taboo defends us against. To investigate and understand it evokes all the resistance-defenses directed against making the taboo conscious, JUST AS THE PATIENT IN THERAPY mobilizes his defenses when analysis comes close to uncovering his unconscious wishes and especially, the oedipal wish.

Freud felt that his own discoveries in Psychoanalysis stood in just such a relationship to the sexual taboos of twentieth-century man. He had *violated* them by questioning their true nature and aroused the anxiety-provoked wrath of civilization seeking to defend itself against its own unconscious impulses which he had correctly explained. Behind even the most intellectually sophisticated defenses of civilized morality lurked the repressed primitive instincts of humanity; and the German philosopher Immanuel Kant's "categorical imperative," the assertion that rational men intuitively understand right from wrong and good from evil, differs in no way from the most primitive "Thou shalt not."

The interwoven strands of totemism and its taboos symbolize and preserve the memory of some historical experience. But like the dream thoughts, the memory of this experience has undergone profound alterations and distortions. How did Freud discover the real nature of that historical experience and in what relationship does it stand to the phenomenon of totemism AND contemporary institutions as well? In answer Freud introduced his theory of the PRIMAL HORDE which is the core of the cultural theories of Psychoanalysis.

Primal Horde

Although the most up-to-date ethological evidence (Ethology: the study of animal behavior in its natural habitat) suggests that the specific observation from which Freud drew his momentous conclusions is invalid (Charles Darwin's notion that gorilla bands were dominated by a jealous male patriarch), it is still pertinent to note that Freud always sought to understand the products of human psychology in a NATURALISTIC-EVOLUTIONARY manner. The theory of the PRIMAL HORDE is one of science's first major efforts at understanding the institutions of human civilization in terms of man's biological heritage.

In pre-historic times men lived in small bands dominated by an all-powerful male, much in the manner of baboon troops. This patriarch jealously guarded his sexual prerogatives with the females of the Primal Horde and when the younger males became of age they were either expelled or castrated. (Perhaps this castration Freud speaks of may be considered more psychological than physical. The father would then have reduced the sons of the horde to sexual impotence through the force of his authority rather than literally castrating them; although, the widespread practice of circumcision which in Psychoanalysis symbolizes castration might lend credence to a more literal reading of Freud's hypothesis.) The father of the horde was the first tyrant.

It must be remembered that Freud is compressing, into a description of a single happening, events which took generations to unfold and which were repeated many times by independent groups of pre-historic men. (The evidence of world mythology suggested to Freud the reoccurrence of the events narrated by him as a single happening.) Then, at a given moment in the history of the horde, probably when the old male had passed his physical prime, the expelled brothers of the horde led by the youngest son who must have reached maturity just at the time of the father's incipient decline, banded together and killed him. The brothers then ate the body of the father (cannibalism) in order to incorporate his power and authority. Primitive warriors still avoid certain animals like the rabbit whose flesh used as food might make them timid, and seek rather to feed on powerful and courageous animals.

Upon the death of the father who had prohibited sexual activity within his group, there followed the dissolution of all the taboos that he had so strictly enforced and especially the prohibition against INCEST. An epoch of communal promiscuity followed.

The father was dead but "Long live the father." This event Freud argued was the genesis of HUMAN PSYCHOLOGY as Psychoanalysis discovers it to be, with the inception of the dynamics of Repression, Unconscious Memories, Guilt, Resistance against recalling the deed, Renunciation, the Incest Taboo and the first Compromise-Formations.

Though consciously forgotten, the unconscious memory of the deed and the murdered father's prohibitions began to return collectively to the brothers. This constituted the first historical instance of the phenomenon typically associated with the neurosis, the *Return of the Repressed*, the tendency which repressed unconscious memories of forbidden wishes and deeds possess to press forward toward consciousness. They are of course vigorously repulsed and denied direct access to consciousness but their activity results in the formation of the numerous psychic compromises we have already discussed.

Totem as Religion

The brothers had *denied by forgetting* their momentous deed of parricide. They had *collectively repressed* its memory. They had violated the father's taboo against Incest with the sisters of the horde. But as the *unconscious memory* slowly returned to them, pressing forward toward consciousness charged with the castration anxiety associated with the forbidden deeds, the first Compromise-Formations in the history of human psychology came about. The brothers had hated the father for his sexual prohibitions. But they had also revered and loved him. Ambivalence had existed BEFORE the inception of civilized psychology.

Slowly the positive attitude toward the father and the remorse associated with the vaguely dawning recollection of the deed led the brothers to RENOUNCE THE SISTERS OF THE HORDE AND RE-INSTITUTE the murdered father's incest taboo, and elevate his memory to the cherished figure of the symbolic animal ancestor of the horde (Clan). ALL THIS WAS DONE UNCONSCIOUSLY and signaled the beginning of religion (in its totemic form), sexual morality (based on the Incest taboo), and the whole psychology of civilized man.

It initiated the triumph of the Reality Principle (the Father's will) over the Pleasure Principle (Incest with the sisters). But it also activated the power of creative imagination in men, as they sought to commemorate in their myths and religious practices BOTH THE DEED AND ITS DENIAL.

In renouncing the sisters of the horde the brothers established the first moral taboos, *Thou Shalt Not Marry Thy Sister* and *Thou Shalt Not Murder Thy Father,* although the second taboo was not consciously couched in language which came too close to recalling the reality of the Primal Deed. But human Ambivalance could not settle for such a simple solution and so while both taboos were respected and enforced, THEY WERE ALSO LITERALLY AS WELL AS SYMBOLICALLY VIOLATED! The brothers of the horde submitted to the unconscious memory of the castrating father's will and following the interim of incestuous sexual permissiveness, renounced their sisters. But they also rebelled against these twin-taboos in the institution of the practices of totemism. The totem-animal (symbolizing the father of the Primal Horde) is revered *AND* KILLED AND EATEN. The females of the clan are Taboo but at the time of the totem festival, INCEST IS REQUIRED. THE PRACTICES OF TOTEMISM ARE THE FIRST CELEBRATIONS AND COMMEMORATIONS of the murder of the father of the Primal Horde and the violation of his sexual taboos. But they are far from being the only ones.

Totem and Taboo in Mythology and Literature

The mythologies of the peoples of the world are structured according to the same unconscious requirements. So are certain pre-Judeo-Christian religious and moral practices. Great literature also celebrates the event. A few examples will underscore the omnipresence of these themes.

Classical Greek, Roman and Norse mythologies relate similar tales of the incestuous marriage of brother and sister Gods after the overthrow of a tyrant. Zeus overthrows his father Kronos, CASTRATES him, and releases his brothers and sisters from imprisonment whereupon they intermarry. Among the Romans it was Jupiter who did the same to his father Saturn. In ancient Egypt, the paraoh was REQUIRED to marry his blood sister and the great scholar Immanuel Velikovsky (himself trained as a Freudian psychoanalyst) has written a convincing book (*Oedipus and Akhnaton*, 1960) to prove that King Oedipus of Thebes in Greece (from whence the term Oedipus Complex derives) was in fact the religious revolutionary pharaoh Akhnaton who actually married his mother. Along with the Oedipus tale, Freud listed Dostoyevsky's *Brothers Karamazov* and Shakespeare's *Hamlet* as the greatest works in Western literature and all three deal directly with the themes of parricide and incest. The Peruvian Incas practiced royal incestuous marriage and the Trobriand Islanders of New Guinea trace their descent from the intermarriage of brother and sister and the overthrow of a tyrannical "uncle." The Norse Nibelungenlied and Richard Wagner's operas known as the Ring Cycle depict the birth of a new morality of love in the world which springs from a brother-sister union which in Wagner's work is the CAUSE of the downfall of the patriarchal morality of the Gods. The typical hero of Greek tragedy usually commits some bloody deed for which he must atone. While the parricide-incest theme is not clearly evident in all instances of the genre, Freud argued that the tragic hero symbolizes the youngest son of the Primal Horde who led his brothers in revolt against the father and is punished for the deed while the brothers (the Chorus) deny any complicity in the deed. The word tragedy itself evokes that past. Although it is disputed, some argue that it derives etymologically from the classic word *Traigos* (goat), and the goat was the symbol of the patron God of tragedy Dionysus. There is evidence that goats were sacrificed at the tragic festivals and the well-known Hebrew practice of finding a "scape-goat" for the sins of the community (the brothers' sins) and ritually killing it points to the same event, both re-living and denying the event, but at the same time gaining pardon from the father.

The psychoanalytic explanation of the genesis of culture possesses far-reaching implications for an understanding of the whole of human history. Mankind has not been allowed "a moment's rest" since the fatal deed. A process of historical dialectic has unfolded since the events of the Primal Horde and the development of history, society and politics has hewn close to the lines of the original pre-historic occurrences. This dialectic (not to be confused with either the logical dialectic of Plato or the historical dialectic of Marx) can be viewed as the unending alternation between periods of freedom and periods of repression, rejection of the Primal father's will and acceptance of it. The swings of this dialectical pendulum are caused by the universal unconscious memory traces of his murder and different epochs in history are to be understood in terms of just how much of the collectively Repressed memories have returned.

Judaism/Christianity and the Primal Horde

In addition to the Pre-Judeo-Christian mythological conceptions discussed above Freud sought the explanation of both Judaism and Christianity and their peculiar interdependence and inter-relationship in the dialectic of the Primal Horde. The psychologically remarkable phenomenon of anti-Semitism keenly interested Freud, who all his life was fiercely proud of his ethnic Jewish heritage (though rejecting the religious paraphernalia of his people). Both religions hold as canonical the familiar tale, in Chapter

3 of *Genesis*, of the expulsion of Adam and Eve from the Garden of Eden for disobedience to the will of God the Father. The Eden myth is echoed in all ancient speculations about a Golden Age. The expulsion myth contains, in distorted form, of course, the historical memory of the primal crime. From *Genesis* 2 and 3 the nature of the crime as parricidal-sexual is clear. The first self-conscious awareness of both Adam and Eve (after they have *eaten* of the fruit of the tree of knowledge of good and evil; i.e., cannibalized the father) is of their nakedness and they are overcome with sexual shame and sew on fig leaves. Yet, the author of *Genesis* 2 felt required, in the last verse of that chapter, to emphasize that the man and woman were naked and WERE NOT ashamed. It is only after knowledge of good and evil (the return of the repressed memories of the primal father's taboos on incestuous intercourse) that shame results. Further evidence for the sexual nature of the crime is the serpent, a universal phallic symbol. Eve is cursed in her "conception and child bearing," another hint.

The historical relationship existing between Judaism and Christianity is paradoxical. On the one hand, Judaism is spiritually the "parent" religion, and Christianity is its offspring. It has been argued too, that Judaism is much more of a religion of the "father," while in Christianity, the figure of "the son" plays a much more prominent role. But these religions may also be viewed in the familiar relationship of older to younger brother, since both share one Father-God and one Holy Bible, the Old Testament. The Jewish assertion of being a people "chosen" by God the Father for preferential treatment would be the source of unconscious jealous hostility by the "younger brother" religion, which then asserts that the religion of the son has in many ways superseded the religion of the father.

Christ as Totem-Figure

The crucial line of division between the two religions is, of course, the figure of Jesus Christ, whom Freud viewed as a symbol of the youngest son who led the brothers in the overcoming of the father. Jesus is sacrificed to the memory of the father's will by the company of brothers as atonement for their "sins," crimes which can only be construed as murders. Jesus atones for all mankind's complicity in the murder of the primal father. But at the same time HE BECOMES ONE SUBSTANCE with God the father, i.e., replaces him. The brothers (the followers of Christ, Christians) literally eat their God, Jesus, in the cannibalistic act of Holy Communion, again a commemoration of primal cannibalism, because while Jesus is the son of God, he has also become God the Father. It is to be carefully noted that in many sects of Christianity, including the most powerful, Roman Catholicism, the eating of the communion wafer is the literal act of eating God's body and drinking his blood. (The miracle of Transubstantiation, which is the heart of the Catholic Mass, literally transforms bread and wine into the body and blood of Jesus.) It is as if the Christian were saying (unconsciously of course) that "Yes, we killed the father but we admit it and atone for it by the sacrifice of our leader who then replaces the murdered God. You Jews do not confess to the primal crime, hence, you are still being punished for it."

Judaism and Circumcision

It is the central ritual of Judaism, circumcision, which evokes unconscious memories of the Primal Father as source of castration-anxiety since circumcision has the unconscious meaning of castration. But circumcision was not limited to the Hebrews in the ancient world. The Egyptians practiced it centuries before Christ. So do many primitive African and Asian peoples. The widespread use of circumcision indicates a vivid commemoration of the will of the primal father.

We first encounter circumcision in the Jewish tradition in the story of Abraham and Isaac wherein the first patriarch is commanded by God the Father to sacrifice his first born child, but then relents and introduces this substitute form of castration as a sign of the covenant between himself and his people. The Jews have accepted the will of the father and received his special favor by a symbolic form of self-castration. The same is of course true for all other cultures which practice this rite.

Anti-Semitism

But the Gentile nations, Rome and Greece, abhorred the practice, which is the principal reason why St. Paul rejected physical circumcision as a necessity for inclusion within the covenant that God had made with man. The Greeks and Romans would not have accepted the practice of mutilation of the genitals. Certain difficulties appear in Freud's explanation of the practice of circumcision as THE PRINCIPAL CAUSE of the phenomenon of anti-Semitism, especially since large portions of the contemporary world have come to accept the practice (for allegedly hygienic rather than religious reasons). Be that as it may, Psychoanalysis' unconscious equation circumcision = castration would aggravate and stir up all the unconscious anxieties in the uncircumcised which surround the central masculine fear, castration-anxiety. These anxieties can (and often did) result in outbreaks of murderous rage directed at those who symbolically represent and remind the uncircumcised of their deepest unconscious fears. Freud found the conscious superficial explanations for anti-Semitism to be in the form of unconscious rationalizations of castration-anxiety, and totally incapable of explaining the magnitude and ferocity of this phenomenon. It may or may not have been the case that International Jewish finance was the cause of Germany's defeat in World War I. It may or may not have been (or be) the case that Jews fill up the desirable professions, that they gain an economic superiority wherever they go through sharp business practices or by "sticking together," or that they consider themselves Jews first and citizens of their adopted homeland second. None of these explanations can account for the near-genocide of the Jews by the Nazis in the 1930's and 1940's. And in reading Hitler's *Mein Kampf*, the bible of anti-Semitism, one again encounters wildly irrational fears of "blood-contamination" of the pure Aryan by the "dirty Jew." Blood-defilement is equivalent in the unconscious to syphilophobia; and Hitler and his followers were for the most part sexual psychopaths. Anti-Semitism is the result of unconscious castration-anxiety on the part of sexually sick minds.

Freud and Marxism

In his judgment of the most important historical force of our time, International Communism (Marxism), Freud showed his usual ambivalence. He once thought that Marxism might succeed in establishing a far greater degree of human happiness than patriarchal capitalism. But after the USSR (see: W. Reich: *The Sexual Revolution*, for details), and his own discovery of what he believed to be the all-pervasive Death Instinct, Freud rejected the notion that deliberate rational planning could produce a social order consonant with human instinctual demands. It is NOT the institution of Private Property that causes human aggressiveness as the Marxists assert. The Aggressive Instinct long preceded the acquisiton of private property and, far from being a socially acquired element in human nature, it is one of mankind's most basic drives. The Marxist-Utopian schemes (echoes of the post-primal-horde freedom of the brothers) collapsed into the repressive nightmare of Stalinism (the return of the repressed father's will). All Utopian schemes are doomed to failure and the threat of extinction lies heavily on the whole of human civilization.

Dialectic of History

Throughout human history this pattern has repeated itself innumerable times, in both the great and small events of civilization. This is the blueprint of the Freudian Dialectic of History:

1. A repressive, tyrannical regime, directed by a dictator, emperor, a political party, absolute statism, representing the will of the primal father.

2. This regime is then violently overthrown by revolutionary-utopian thinkers who dream of a better lot for mankind and actually seek to implement their schemes. This is the period of the freedom of the brothers in the post-primal horde condition.

3. All Utopian schemes founder on the rock of human instincts. A violent reaction sets in, freedom is again stifled and AN EVEN MORE REPRESSIVE REGIME THAN THE ONE OVERTHROWN comes into power. Here we see the Return of the Repressed father's will.

We have discussed the re-enactment of this drama in the yearly rituals of totemic religions, wherein the totem animal (father) was killed and eaten and all incest taboos abandoned, only to be reinstated at the termination of the festal period.

The festivals of civilized men bear this same mark. The puritanical Romans celebrated the Saturnalia on the 25th of December, the birthday of Saturn. Promiscuity and drunkenness were the order of the day. The Comic Festivals of the ancient Greeks held in the Spring of each year were frankly obscene, and the plays of Aristophanes bear witness to this bawdy interlude in the lives of the relatively well-behaved Greeks. In modern times, we have the Latin Mardi Gras, and Carnival time. These festivals signal the removal of year-round moral prohibitions but upon their termination, the old standards are once again strictly enforced. (It is significant that Lent follows the Mardi Gras; it is a time of severe abstemiousness and personal sacrifice.)

Modern Revolution and Freudian Dialectic

A glance at the history of modern political revolutions supplies further testimony for the existence of the Unconscious Dialectic of History (not to be confused with the Marxist Dialectic of History to which it bears no resemblance). We may begin with the Puritan Revolution in England in the middle of the seventeenth century. This upheaval followed hard upon the heels of a period of licentiousness known as the Elizabethan Age, the time of Shakespeare. As its name implies, and as we have come to know it from our own history, Puritanism was a system of rigidly enforced moral taboos directed against most pleasurable activities. When the British threw the Puritans out and restored the monarchy, the period of their history known as the Restoration, moral prohibitions were again relaxed; and, as we see in Henry Fielding's novel *Tom Jones,* promiscuity was somewhat the order of the day in all social classes. But, within a century and a half, the most repressive-moralistic reign since the 1640's dominated British consciousness for the last three-quarters of the nineteenth century. This was the Victorian age in which Freud was born and worked and the term itself has become synonymous with sexual repression and moral hypocrisy. Two world wars amashed Great Britain as a world power and following the second great war, straight-laced England disappeared and its place was taken by the Beatles, Carnaby Street and the mini-skirt.

The French Revolution was made in the name of Liberty, Equality, and Fraternity, the Rights of Man, and the ideals of brotherhood and it inspired deeds of nobility and sacrifice. But its high ideals could not be sustained and the revolution degenerated into the bloody reign of Robespierre and finished with the French submitting themselves to a more absolute dictator than any Bourbon King: Napoleon Bonaparte.

The same psychological cycle dominated the Russian Revolution of 1917 which overthew the Czar Nicholas (to whom the Russians referred as their "little father") and which actually gave the Russian people their first and only democratic regime led by the liberal Alexander Kerensky. But he in turn was overthrown by Vladimir Lenin who lived to see the failure of the socialist ideals of brotherhood and sexual freedom in the Soviet Union. Upon the death of Lenin, the entire revolutionary fabric collapsed and was succeeded by the absolute rule of the bloodiest tyrant in mankind's history, Joseph Stalin.

Accurate parallels may be drawn with the Chinese, Cuban, and other socialist revolutions of this century. First, a repressive political regime; second, the revolt of the idealists against the established authority and the destruction of the Establishment (the will of the father) but finally, the failure of revolutionary hopes and the re-establishment of a more repressive Establishment than the one overthrown by the revolution.

Uniqueness of American Revolution

For totally non-chauvinistic reasons the American Revolution must be excepted from the dialectic. It provides an instructive example of how a conservative revolution differs from the radical revolution described above. A conservative revolution does not seek to sweep away the *Ancien Régime* (old order) and replace it with a Utopian society BOUND BY THE FREUDIAN DIALECTIC OF HISTORY TO INEVITABLE FAILURE! As its name implies, a conservative revolution seeks to *conserve* the old order (will of the father), but also, to be included within the social, political, and legal guarantees of that order. Though there were plenty of political radicals around in 1775, for the most part the colonists did not wish to overthrow the King and Parliament as their Puritan ancestors had done in 1642. (The Puritans executed King Charles I, reenacting the murder of the primal horde father.) They wished simply to be assured the rights of Englishmen which they felt themselves to be. The American Revolution did not commence with the assertion of a new social order but with the demand to be included within the old one. Events led to quite a different outcome, but, even in the making of a new government, the founding fathers were guided in their thinking by one of the most conservative (as opposed to radical) political theories of their time, the philosopher John Locke's *Second Essay on Civil Government.*

This historical digression has been undertaken in order to show how Freud's theory of the Primal Horde accurately reflects many major political developments in Western history.

"Group Psychology and the Analysis of the Ego" (1921)

In the second application of the Primal Horde theory to an understanding of social and political phenomena, Freud entered the field of Social Psychology for the first time in an attempt to explain psychoanalytically the relationship which exists between a group and its leader. Freud uses the same German word "Masse" in this work as he does in the last essay in *Totem and Taboo.* In the latter work, the word *Masse* has usually been translated "Horde." But the word "Horde" in English conjures up the idea of an enormous number of human beings, whereas the Primal "Horde" was quite the opposite. It was a small band or "group" (Masse) of proto-human beings. The Primal Horde thus is to be understood as the Primal Group, and it is the same Primal Group mentality that Freud undertakes to analyze in the current work.

Group Psychology and the Analysis of the Ego refuted the criticism of opponents who claimed that Psychoanalysis was individual psychology *only*, and hence, could tell us little or nothing about the actions of individuals on a social scale. Freud answered by asserting that, since individual psychology is ALWAYS in some way bound up with relations to others, Psychoanalysis is most definitely a social psychology. But Freud's explanation of the actions of individuals in groups provides us with a profound insight into what has become the principal form of social behavior in the twentieth century. With the advent of Fascism, Communism, and all other variations of political absolutism, the burning question how can a SINGLE MAN acquire the unquestioned rule over millions of his fellow men becomes perhaps the most vital social issue of our time.

Of course, one-man rule has occurred throughout the centuries, in Eastern civilizations, the Roman Empire, the Medieval Catholic Church, and in the modern nation-states of Spain, France and England, to mention but a few examples. But never has one-man rule reached the scale and magnitude of its twentieth-century manifestations. Besides, it has been argued that mankind has made political "progress" in our century. If true, then the relapse into absolutism and its companion barbarism must be explained as a mass example of REGRESSION TO UNCONSCIOUS, INFANTILE MODES OF BEHAVIOR. And this is precisely how Freud does explain modern political absolutism.

The "Leader" and the Masses

The "Leader" (Führer, Duce, Party Boss) is the key to the psychoanalytic comprehension of such regressive modes of behavior. The role played by the leader in the COLLECTIVE PSYCHE of his followers cannot be accounted for on rational grounds; indeed, successful leaders are conscious of the necessity of appealing to, and capturing the IRRATIONAL needs, desires and fears of the group. Hence, though he himself is not aware of the precise nature of his authority, he is in fact appealing to the UNCONSCIOUS, REPRESSED, INFANTILE GROUP MIND which his followers share in common, and in which they participate. The leader is the unconscious heir to the mantle of the primal father. He inherits his absolute power and unquestioned authority and his followers (the sons) are, as a group, incapable of rational criticism and independent judgment in matters concerning the leader's will. (The Führer *is* the will of the German people; Il Duce is always *right;* Marxist-Leninist doctrine is *not* subject to Revisionism, The Sayings of Chairman Mao, etc.) The group responds to its leader as each individual member did to his personal father in childhood, and as the sons of the Primal Group responded to the Primal Father. Obedience to his will signifies psychological castration. The group hungers for the approval of the leader and carries out his absolute commands without regard to any personal, moral judgments. The group is actually in a waking-state of hypnosis.

Infantilism of the Group

While the group imperatively needs the leader, his power over them is signified by the crucial psychological difference that he does not need the group. (That is, psychologically he is independent of them, though of course he needs them as an instrument for carrying out his will.) The group "identifies" the leader as its collective EGO-IDEAL or conscience, and his will is the source of all judgments of right and wrong. This regression to infantile mental functioning and total dependence on the father-leader relieves the followers of both the necessity for making independent judgments AND the sense of responsibility and guilt for the consequences of their actions; this is the reason why groups are capable of incredible acts of barbarism as well as acts of heroism, idealism, and sacrifice. But their actions are completely dominated by the Primary Processes of the unconscious and all the restraints imposed upon individual behavior by Repression of the instincts are abrogated. The group is invincible. The group is always right. Because the leader-father tells it so.

Words as Magic

The leader is able to impose his monomaniacal will on the group which lacks a coherent will of its own and is vulnerable to the mass psychological manifestations of *suggestibility* and *contagion*. The major instrument by which the leader gains *hypnotic control* over his followers, is the spoken word, of which he is a master. Words are magic to the followers who fall under the spell of what Freud, in the third essay of *Totem and Taboo,* called "The omnipotence of thought." The belief in the all-powerful influence of mental processes links neurosis and social psychology since the behavior of both individual neurotics, and social groups is determined by the conviction that words, thoughts and ideas are as real as physical objects. The "omnipotence of thought" presents us with the universal phenomenon of the overvaluation of psychological reality as opposed to physical reality. This is why groups can be led to accept all kinds of patent absurdities from their leaders. It is not physical reality that determines group action but rather the Primary Process which the leader knows intuitively how to manipulate through verbal magic. This intuitive knowledge of the group mind is the true source of political leadership. It gives us the reason why so many Germans could accept the near-psychotic delusion of a Master Race theory. Hitler's theory supplied the fulfillment of an unconscious wish to his followers whose rational faculties were literally paralyzed when their unconscious fantasies and anxieties were mobilized by the most demonic orator of modern times. Freud defined this phenomenon as "... mistaking an ideal process for a real one." Rational considerations for the truth of ideas are submerged in unconscious wish-fulfillments. And for Freud, most political theory and activity is merely the rationalization of unconscious group wishes which are the "truly operative and real" wellsprings of social action.

Freud describes magical suggestibility under hypnosis, in much neurotic and psychotic behavior, in the normal condition of being in love, AND in mass political behavior as "... an irreducible primitive phenomenon, a fundamental fact in the mental life of man." Any political or social group is bound together by the energy of the Libido which Freud now terms, after the philosopher Plato, Eros. EROS FUNCTIONS AS THE MOST HIGHLY SUBLIMATED FORM OF LIBIDO. It is the energetic source of all group behavior. But sublimated Eros is aim-inhibited, that is, its original object is renounced in favor of the Ego-Ideal. Whereas Libido cathects (charges with energy) first the mother and then a person of the opposite sex, Eros (the sublimated form of Libido) becomes the cement which holds the group together BUT AT THE EXPENSE OF PERSONAL, LIBIDINAL GRATIFICATION, and its energies derive from the repression and consequent inhibition of sexual satisfaction.

Groups of any kind, then, are formed on two principles:

1. The introjection of a common ego-ideal; the person of the leader.

2. Eros, the aim-inhibited sexual instinct, which supplies the "energy" by which the group holds together. This energy is totally de-sexualized Libido, and excepted from the demands of mature, genital, individual sexuality.

"Moses and Monotheism" (1938-39)

Not only did Freud never abandon (nor even severely modify) his Primal Horde theory, but it was to be the very last theme which concerned him in the final year of his life and produced, a quarter of a century after its initial formulation, his last contribution to psychoanalytic speculation, *Moses and Monotheism*. The book was written in two parts. The first half was composed in Vienna and was not published until Freud, fleeing the Nazi occupation of Austria in 1938 and finding asylum in England, completed the second half of the book and presented the world with the astounding deduction that the greatest of all Jewish historical figures was NOT A JEW AT ALL BUT AN EGYPTIAN!

As in all of his incursions into scientific, literary and scholarly fields not his own, Freud derived the first insight into this rather bizarre hypothesis from a recognized authority in the field of biblical studies, the scholar Ernst

Sellin. Sellin's claim, according to Freud, was that there existed within the Jewish tradition (though not within the Bible itself) evidence to indicate that the Jews had murdered their greatest prophet Moses! It is still a matter of confusion whether Sellin did or did not assert this and, if he did, whether or not he later retracted the statement. The details of the controversy may be found in the third volume of Jones' biography of Freud. But whether or not Freud's mind had taken this turn because of external influences, the hypothesis and its demonstration became his own. As usual, he plunged into the deeper layers of the problem and employed the techniques of Psychoanalysis to elucidate hidden material which could never have been recovered employing the tools of biblical scholarship alone. The theory of the Primal Horde was to prove the key to a deeper understanding of the Jewish people and their history.

Here, as in the book on the life of Leonardo da Vinci which will be examined later, Freud played the master detective. He felt that in the case of both these works, his deductions would stand or fall on the psychoanalytic interpretation of the evidence he had collated and on whether alternative explanations could produce a more feasible conclusion than his own. In anticipation of our discussion of the Leonardo monograph, it is well to remark that for either hypothesis, the bits and pieces of evidence taken separately can produce convincing and much less spectacular conclusions than Freud's.

The question that must be decided by the student in both cases (and in judging the whole of Psychoanalysis as well) is whether the mosaic constructed by Freud from a wide variety of seemingly unrelated clues is the best possible interpretation of the Leonardo and Moses stories. Whether, to remain with our metaphor of Freud as a master detective, when all the evidence is presented and we have arrived at the concluding page of the detective story, it is the butler and only the butler who could have committed the crime.

Freud's Hypothesis: Part One

Moses was an Egyptian priest of the great pharaoh Ikhnaton (or Akhnaton) who reigned in the middle of the fourteenth century B.C. and is widely recognized by Egyptologists as the first monotheist in history, that is, the first known historical personage to proclaim the existence of a single God, or, at least, a single supreme God. As was earlier mentioned, Ikhnaton has been identified by Immanuel Velikovsky as the living source of the Oedipus legend. After the mid-nineteenth century (A.D.) discovery of the ruins of Ikhanaton's capitol city at Tel-El-Amarna in Egypt, it is clear that this man indeed ranks as a revolutionary figure in the history of religion. He rejected the polytheistic pantheon of the ancient Egyptians and replaced the myriad animal-gods with his single Deity, Aton, symbolized by the disc of the sun, to whom he composed a number of religious hymns strikingly similar to some of the best known Old Testament psalms. But upon his death the hereditary priest caste of Egypt sought to efface his memory and destroy all vestiges of the new religion, and literally nothing was known of the pharaoh Ikhnaton until less than a century ago.

Other Evidence

From this scant information Freud began to build his thesis that Moses was an Egyptian who brought the religion of monotheism and the custom of circumcision to the Hebrews. But other factual evidence exists around which Freud wove his strange speculations.

1. The suffix "mose" appears in many Egyptian names, for instance, the well known Tut-mose.

2. According to the Hebrew legend, Moses was raised as an Egyptian prince in the house of the pharaoh. The biblical narrative tells of the pharaoh's daughter finding the infant in the bullrushes and raising him as her own. But Freud, who was fond of quoting Jewish-

humor, related the tale of an astute Jewish lad who, upon hearing the Moses story for the first time, that is, that the pharaoh's daughter was not the mother of Moses remarked, "That's what *she* said." The process of "reversal into its opposite," which we have seen to be a basic law of the Primary Process, occurs here in a unique manner. World mythologies always have the Hero of a given people being born into a noble family and then exiled to a humble one from which he returns to assert his birthright. In the Moses myth, the tendentious process has been reversed and Moses is separated from humble origins (among the enslaved Hebrews) and raised as a noble. The purpose of this "reversal into its opposite" (which is of course unconscious) is to guarantee the Jewishness of Moses and the authenticity of the "chosen people."

3. The essential Jewish practice of circumcision, which the Old Testament claims as a sign of uniqueness and divine favor, was practiced by the Egyptians as well as many primitive cultures. Circumcision would certainly be a peculiar "sign of the covenant," between God and the people of Abraham, since it could in no way distinguish the Hebrew from the Egyptian, Phoenician, Syrian and primitive peoples completey removed from any contact with the pre-historic Mediterranean world.

4. Moses is said to have "stuttered." He required an interpreter, his brother Aaron, when speaking to the people. Freud's inference is that Moses did not speak Hebrew easily.

5. The spiritually sophisticated concept of Monotheism would be difficult to explain as the product of rough desert tribesmen in bondage to a powerful civilization. So would the theme of the return of a redemptive Messiah which Freud suggests adds weight to the unwritten tradition that:

6. The Jews murdered Moses, suffered great guilt, and longed for his return.

Freud's Motives

Hostile critics have argued that Freud sought to kill his own "Jewishness" by "killing" Moses (a surrogate father) as a Jew, i.e., making him an Egyptian. This ingenious hypothesis is just plain silly. Throughout his lifetime Freud was fiercely proud of being a Jew. His books were among the first to be burned by the Nazis when they came to power and Hitler called Psychoanalysis the "Jewish" science. It has also been suggested that the book *Totem and Taboo*, without doubt the spiritual "father" of *Moses and Monotheism*, does not reveal the origin of human morals in general, but rather, the specifically Jewish morality. The first paragraph of *Moses and Monotheism* belies this unfounded assertion. Freud knew exactly what he was doing in "depriving a people of its greatest leader," especially since he identified himself as one of those people. One may legitimately assume that Freud, of all people, would have carefully scrutinized his own motives for writing the Moses book. It is also germane to an understanding of Freud's ethnic identification that he refused to accept any royalties for the Hebrew translation of *Totem*. (He was also a member of B'nai Brith.)

Freud's Hypothesis: Part Two

The Egyptian Moses, imbued with the fervid consciousness of his dead master Ikhnaton, cast about for some means of perpetuating the religion of Monotheism. The Hebrews, a rough desert people, were at that time in bondage (either as slaves or paid laborers) in Egypt. Moses CHOSE the Hebrews to be the inheritors of Ikhnaton's religion and led them out of bondage. They were literally a "chosen" people, an event unique in the history of the world's religions. As a physical sign of this choice, Moses imposed the Egyptian custom of circumcision on the Hebrews, an unconscious traumatic reminder of the Primal Horde. (Of course, the introduction of this custom was later projected far back beyond the time of Moses to the time of Abraham, an unconscious distortion which served to conceal the true originator of this crucial act and also, his untimely fate.)

The rebellious and stiff-necked Hebrews rejected the new faith which imposed severe restrictions on sensuality and pleasure in the name of the will of God-The-Father (more echoes of the Primal Horde situation) and revolted and KILLED MOSES. This act, the repetition of the murder of the father of the Primal Horde, indelibly impressed itself on Jewish consciousness (technically, on Jewish "unconsciousness"), and, combined with the powerfully symbolic reminder, the ritual of circumcision, which it will be remembered is a substitute form of castration, the fate imposed by the Primal Father on his sons, forever set the Jews apart from the rest of the human race. THE MURDER OF MOSES WAS THE RE-ENACTMENT OF THE MURDER OF THE FATHER OF THE PRIMAL HORDE! Although the event was repressed and forgotten, just as the horde brothers had repressed and forgotten their deed of parricide, after some centuries, following the dialectic of the Return of the Repressed, the Jews accepted the absolute will of the One God, The Primal Father, to which they had been reintroduced by the murdered Moses. They developed a morality of renunciation and taboo, especially directed toward sexual things. Because of their unique historical experience, the Jews began to think of themselves as better than other peoples, as chosen by the returned surrogate-father Moses (which, historically speaking, they were). The denial of the repetition of the primal murder upon Moses was incorporated in another crucial article of Judaism, the Messianic hope. The Father-Moses-Messiah would return and re-affirm the status of the Jews as a chosen people. At the same time, the castigations levelled upon the Jewish people by their subsequent history were viewed (unconsciously) as punishment for the Moses-Father murder. When the symbolic figure of Jesus appears and the Jews again reject the will of the returned-Father-Messiah, their fate takes on the peculiar hue of post-Christian epoch anti-Semitism, already discussed. But Freud here adds an interesting corollary to his theory of anti-Semitism. The hatred of Judaism is at bottom a hatred of Christianity, a rebellion against the will of the Primal Horde father!

The institutions of history, culture and civilization are not the result of rational deliberative processes but rather, the outer manifestations of the unconscious dialectic of the collective human psyche. The Primal Horde theory supplies the master key for a comprehension of this process. Every event in contemporary human experience, from the torch light parades in Nuremberg in 1935 to a football rally on the campus of a small American college in 1972, is to be explained by the all-pervading influence of the *Collective Unconscious* (to use a term borrowed from C. G. Jung), the Primary Process which accounts for the existence and nature of humanity's institutions from the time of the Primal Horde. The Primal Horde experience is the very source of the psychoanalytic explanation of human culture.

It was the first, and it remains the most important, application that Freud made of his clinical discoveries to the general problems of civilization. Along with the *Interpretation of Dreams*, and the *Three Essays on the Theory of Sexuality*, Freud always considered *Totem and Taboo* to be one of his most important contributions to human knowledge.

We have moved from the *Clinical* to the *Cultural* in our discussion of the major works, discoveries and theories of Freud. We must now investigate the realm of *Metapsychology*, which binds the clinical-therapeutic practice of Psychoanalysis to its Cultural theories. *Metapsychology* means a complete, comprehensive, scientific theory of the human mind and its functioning. We have already investigated a minor but important connection that Freud made between normal and abnormal mental activity in the *Psychopathology of Everyday Life*.

BORDERS
BOOKS AND MUSIC
2240 E. SUNRISE BLVD
FT. LAUDERDALE FL 33304
(954) 566-6335

STORE: 0124   REG: 04/79   TRAN#: 7157
SALE   01/11/2004   EMP: 01054

NEWSPAPERS

NW T   5.00

          Subtotal   5.00
          FLORIDA 6%   .30
1   Item Total   5.30
          CASH   5.30

01/11/2004 10:16AM

Check our store inventory online
at www.bordersstores.com

Shop online at www.borders.com

may not be returned.
Returned merchandise must be in saleable condition.

BORDERS®

Merchandise presented for return, including sale or marked-down items, must be accompanied by the original Borders store receipt. Returns must be completed within 30 days of purchase. The purchase price will be refunded in the medium of purchase (cash, credit card or gift card). Items purchased by check may be returned for cash after 10 business days.

Merchandise unaccompanied by the original Borders store receipt, or presented for return beyond 30 days from date of purchase, must be carried by Borders at the time of the return. The lowest price offered for the item during the 12 month period prior to the return will be refunded via a gift card.

Opened videos, discs, and cassettes may only be exchanged for replacement copies of the original item.
Periodicals, newspapers, out-of-print, collectible and pre-owned items may not be returned.
Returned merchandise must be in saleable condition.

BORDERS®

Merchandise presented for return, including sale or marked-down items, must be accompanied by the original Borders store receipt. Returns must be completed within 30 days of purchase. The purchase price will be refunded in the medium of purchase (cash, credit card or gift card). Items purchased by check may be returned for cash after 10 business days.

Merchandise unaccompanied by the original Borders store receipt, or presented for return beyond 30 days from date of purchase, must be carried by Borders at the time of the return. The lowest price offered for the item during the 12 month period prior to the return will be refunded via a gift card.

Opened videos, discs, and cassettes may only be exchanged for replacement copies of the original item.
Periodicals, newspapers, out-of-print, collectible and pre-owned items may not be returned.
Returned merchandise must be in saleable condition.

BORDERS®

Three major concerns emerge in Freudian thought after 1920: the exact nature of the instincts, the exact nature of the unconscious and its relation to consciousness, and the future of civilization. Freud himself admitted that the works of this period were highly speculative, tentative attempts to resolve the ultimate issues of philosophical psychology. He did not believe that these speculations bore the weight of evidence or carried the conviction of his earlier clinical and cultural discoveries.

But these highly speculative theories complete the intellectual life of one of humanity's greatest minds. They require careful study.

PART THREE

METAPSYCHOLOGY: THE INSTINCT THEORY

1. *Beyond the Pleasure Principle* (1920)
2. *The Future of an Illusion* (1927)
3. *Civilization and Its Discontents* (1930)

The term "Instinct" is currently in disfavor with most psychologists and psychoanalysts. Yet it remains the nucleus of Freud's theory of the dynamics of the Primary Process. The German word "Trieb," translated as "Instinct" in English, was Freud's term for the energy linked to unconscious mental processes. Cassell's German-English dictionary defines "Trieb" as a driving force, motive power, but also as an instinct. While it might appear that a minuscule point is being belabored, it is vital for the student of Freud to recognize that several essential elements are overlooked when the term "drive" is substituted for the term "instinct."

First: The "Trieb" is *NOT* culturally acquired. It is constitutional, innate, inborn; all members of the human species come into the world with the same drives and instincts. *Second:* The Freudian "Trieb" is not merely a response to an external stimulus. It cannot be caused by external circumstances alone, nor can it be much altered by them. It is hereditary and will appear in the human organism regardless of external stimuli. Of course, it may be very much distorted by the force of external stimuli. But it is neither produced by these external forces, nor can it be made to completely conform to them.

Freud vacillated on the exact nature of the instincts throughout his creative life. But he remained an adamant dualist, whatever particular description he may have given of the instincts at a given time. Instincts operate in ambivalent pairs, contradictory opposites which had to be reconciled to the demands of reality. This view gave birth to Freud's theory of all behavior as a "compromise formation" between opposed and conflicting mental demands.

In his initial formulation of the nature of these instincts-in-conflict Freud distinguished the Ego Instincts from the Sexual Instincts; that is, the unavoidable conflict in living beings between the instinct to survive (ego instincts) and the instinct to reproduce their kind (sexual instincts). Later, Freud came to look on the instincts as emanating, not from two distinct sections of the human psyche, but rather, exclusively from the Ego. This theory he termed the theory of Primary Narcissim, and it was as close as he ever was to come to a belief in the existence of a single, undifferentiated life-energy which was not specifically sexual. In this second formulation, the seeming plurality of the instincts was to be determined solely by the criterion of whether they adhered to the Ego itself (narcissicism, self-love, named for the mythological Greek youth who fell in love with himself), or whether they cathected another person (object-love). This theory of the univocity of the instincts (the belief that ONE BASIC INSTINCT EXISTS, from which all others derive) was short-lived. And it was Freud's final and provocative formulation of the duality and opposition of man's instincts that presents the student of Psychoanalysis with so many difficulties. This was the theory of EROS and THE DEATH INSTINCT.

"Beyond the Pleasure Principle" (1920)

The earlier theories of instinctual opposition had been based on direct clinical observation. But Freud's *final formulation* of the opposition between *Eros* and the *Death Instinct* went far beyond anything that could be directly inspected in human behavior. Still, it is essential for the student of Freud to remember that for him, the Death Instinct was primary and OF MUCH GREATER SIGNIFICANCE THAN ALL THE LIFE INSTINCTS SUMMED UP UNDER THE TERM EROS.

After the year 1917, Freud directed his attention to some seemingly paradoxical facts of human psychology. First, while all human organisms seem to be dominated by the Pleasure Principle, the ceaseless search for pleasure and avoidance of pain, many neurotics engage in what is patently self-destructive, painful behavior. The most dramatic refutation of the omnipotence of the Pleasure Principle in psychic life comes from the phenomenon of MASOCHISM. The masochist actively SEEKS PAIN and we are prompted to say colloquially, though quite inaccurately, to the Masochist PAIN *IS PLEASURE*.

Second, a principal characteristic of all neurosis is that neurotics tend to seek out situations and relationships which compel them to relive the traumatic infantile experiences which made them ill. Freud termed this peculiar phenomenon the REPETITION COMPULSION and it represents in the psychology of the individual what the RETURN OF THE REPRESSED represents in collective psychology. Neurotics labor under the strange compulsion to repeat PAINFUL, THREATENING EXPERIENCES, rather than pleasurable ones, which we would assume to be the rule if the Pleasure Principle dominated psychic life as Freud once argued. Since the Repetition Compulsion contradicted the Pleasure Principle, Freud was led to deduce that some drive or force or energy existed in the unconscious which was INDEPENDENT OF THE PLEASURE PRINCIPLE, a drive more fundamental than the drive for pleasure, a drive which came into constant collision with the Pleasure Principle.

This "something, I know not what," Freud called the DEATH INSTINCT, and it slowly but convincingly usurps the primacy of the life instincts in Freudian theory until it becomes the dominant force in human psychology.

A terminological digression is neccessary here. Freud heartily disliked the coining of terms for his discoveries by anyone else, even his faithful pupils. It was suggested, for instance, that the term "Thanatos" (after the Greek God of Death) be substituted for Death Instinct. Another pupil presented the term "Mortido," from the Latin root word for death. "Destruido' was still another term suggested to Freud as a replacement for the term Death Instinct. Both "Mortido" and "Destruido" bear phonetic resemblances to the term "Libido." But Freud rejected them and spoke only of the Death Instinct, as he had previously rejected the term "Electra Complex" for the female counterpart of the Oedipus Complex. Freud did not believe that the invention of a novel vocabulary in any way indicated the fact of new discoveries.

The concept of the existence of the Death Instinct which first appears in 1920 was never relinquished by Freud until the very last words his pen put to paper in the *Outline of Psychoanalysis* in 1939. It was his final word on the nature of the instincts. We must now investigate what the Death Instinct is and how it operates. What observable evidence can be discerned for the confirmation of this dark hypothesis?

Origins of Death Instinct

It was the clinical problem of Masochism that led Freud to his speculations on the nature and function of the Death Instinct. His first formulation of the theory of Masochism was simple and capable of direct, clinical verification. Masochism, the seeming will-to-suffer, is caused by the frustration of original sadistic-aggressive impulses directed toward the external world. When these sadistic impulses meet their inevitable frustration, they turn back against the Ego itself, and supply the energies of the Super-Ego or moral conscience, energies which are directed against the Ego in the form of self-reproaches and an unconscious sense of guilt. The need to be punished is the result of this redirection of originally sadistic impulses. The aggression originally directed toward the external world is frustrated by the Reality Principle and turns back inward against the Ego. This is the essence of Masochism. But after postulating the existence of an instinct "Beyond the Pleasure Principle," the Death Instinct, Freud found it necessary to revise his initial theory of Masochism and replace it with what he called the theory of PRIMARY MASOCHISM. This theory argues that Masochism is NOT the result of the external frustration of aggression which is then turned back inward against the self but rather is the manifestation of a BASIC WILL-TO-DIE WHICH IS DEFLECTED FROM THE SELF TO THE EXTERNAL WORLD IN THE FORM OF SADISM. The Death Instinct is then no longer the result of the frustration of an initial will to live. Rather, it is the PRIMARY DRIVE in all living organisms, the innate impulse directed toward the reinstatement of the most perfect homeostatic state in which all tensions are finally resolved, the state of non-existence, death. An astounding hypothesis indeed! And it is the shadowy Death Instinct that is the cause of sadism and all forms of aggressive behavior in mankind. From the publication of *Beyond the Pleasure Principle* in the year 1920, the concept of aggression as the first derivative of the Death Instinct assumes a dominant role in Freudian theory, replacing sexuality as the most potentially dangerous dilemma confronting civilization.

Tenuousness of Death Instinct Theory

In strictly biological terms (and Freud leaned heavily upon speculative biology in this essay), not a shred of scientific evidence exists to verify the spectacular hypothesis of the Death Instinct. Yet, Psychoanalysis did discover the lengthy catalog of self-destructive, punitive, self-defeating acts, which are motivated in neurotics and normal alike by an unconscious sense of guilt and the consequent need to be punished.

Freud reverted to his initial physical analogy to explain the final triumph of the Death Instinct, the analogy he had borrowed from Fechner and employed thoroughly in every realm of psychology, the Principle of Constancy and Homeostasis. All living energy-systems seek to maintain an equilibrium between energy ingested and energy discharged. When the energy within any system builds beyond a given threshold, it must be discharged. In humans, the energetic passing beyond this threshold is experienced as tension, discomfort, unpleasure. Instinctual energy requires discharge in order to restore equilibrium. Hunger, thirst, sleep, sex, anger are satisfied through the discharge of accumulated tensions and the re-establishing of the homeostatic balance, a state of non-tension, which is the goal of all organic functioning. REST IS THE GOAL OF MOTION!

If this is the basic law of organismic functioning, then, the ultimate purpose of organic tension is total equilibrium, i.e., the total absence of stimulus to which the organism must respond, i.e., DEATH! Freud writes, "... the purpose of life is death ... each organism finds its own way to death." The *life-sexual-libido* energy of Eros becomes one long detour to death, and life itself becomes a ceaseless struggle between the forces of Eros (within which Freud includes his earlier dichotomies of ego-sexual instincts, and narcissistic-object libidinal instincts), and the inevitably victorious forces of the Death Instinct.

Repetition Compulsion and Anxiety

The nature and purpose of the Repetition Compulsion becomes clearer. The Repetition Compulsion (in the service of the Death Instinct) does not really contradict the Pleasure Principle as first supposed. But it does function independently of it; indeed, it is the prerequisite in mental life for the functioning of the Pleasure Principle. The psychological purpose of the Repetition Compulsion is to *bind energy* (Breuer's "bound" and "tonic" energy) which, if not structured according to the homeostatic needs of the psyche would be experienced as anxiety. The psychological purpose of reliving painful, traumatic experiences is the attempt to GAIN CONTROL OVER THEM, TO BIND THE FREE-FLOATING ENERGIES WHICH WOULD BE EXPERIENCED AS ANXIETIES, AND SUBJECT THEM TO THE DOMINANCE OF THE PLEASURE PRINCIPLE. The neurotic's reliving of the traumatic event (events) in his life, is actually an attempt to retrospectively gain control over them, to master the "tonic" (un-bound) energy and incorporate it as *Ego Syntonic;* that is, compatible with the integrated structure of the Ego as it functions in regard to the demands of the Reality Principle.

The discovery of this mechanism helped Freud to explain the nature of dreams which are not pleasurable wish-fulfillments. The final dimension of the Dream-Work is the attempt at *retrospective mastery in fantasy* of the anxiety linked to repressed dream-thoughts and wishes. The dream seeks to gain control over the unresolved unconscious ideas, complexes and wishes and the conflicts they generate, and by so doing, diminish or eliminate the unpleasure which accompanies these impulses. If psychic energy cannot be discharged realistically OR in fantasy, then it must be bound and somehow incorporated in the personality. Seen from this point of view, the Repetition Compulsion is not a psychological exception to the demands for unitary functioning at all. Its existence indicated to Freud that the basic dynamic of mental functioning is not simply the search for pleasure and the modification of this search by the requirements of reality; but rather, the attempt to bind and control ALL energies of the psyche within the structure of an Ego-Syntonic system, a coherent system of mental functions which is oriented in part toward reality, is in part a compromise, in part a network of defenses, and in part fantasy-oriented. It is this last part of the psychology of men which remains purely under the dominance of the Pleasure Principle, while the first three elements perform their functions according to the demands of culture and civilization.

Beyond the Pleasure Principle is a gloomy book but by no means Freud's last word on the nature and destiny of civilization. He had one final doomsday book to write, *Civilization and Its Discontents*.

We may call *Totem and Taboo* the *Alpha* of the psychoanalytic theory of culture, telling us how civilization got to be as it is. *Civilization and Its Discontents* is the *Omega* of the Freudian theory of human institutions, his last word on the future prospects and possibilities of civilization. It stands as one of the most potent condemnations of civilization ever conceived.

"The Future of an Illusion" (1927)

But in the middle of this gloomy period of Freud's speculations on the nature and fate of human institutions appeared a little book in which he cast an analytic eye on the phenomenon of religion. As we have already seen, Freud's interest in the problems of religion extended from the genetic studies in *Totem and Taboo* to his last book on any subject, *Moses and Monotheism,* a period of 25 years. *The Future of an Illusion* appeared about halfway between these two major works, and in it, Freud condemned what he took to be mankind's sturdiest crutch, organized religion.

But this essay also deals with the fate of culture, as do all of Freud's major non-clinical works of the 1920's. It has been noted that Freud considered himself a "cheerful pessimist" in matters regarding the human condition. But in the three works under discussion in this section, there is very little "cheerfulness" in evidence, and an increasing degree of "pessimism." It was during this period of his life (Freud reached his 70th birthday in 1926) that he un-

derwent a series of agonizing and only partially successful
operations for cancer of the jaw. Some critics account for
Freud's increasing literary pessimism by the degree of suffering he underwent during this period, and the natural
inclination of an aging and seriously ill man of genius to
turn his thought to what seemed to be rapidly approaching end and the insubstantial vanity of all things human.
It was also during this time that Freud lost several loved
ones and so it is understandable, this line of criticism goes,
that death would more and more preoccupy his mind.

Be that as it may, Freud never lost his tone of strict objectivity in dealing with the cultural problems confronted
during this time, and nowhere do we find anything of a personal note injected into the discussion. Despite his personal physical and emotional agonies, Freud's intelligence
and judgment remained lucid and his capacity to render a
persuasive argument in the finest literary style unimpaired.

Freud and Religion

The Future of an Illusion views religion as one of the
major institutional wish-fulfillments which enables men
to tolerate the demands for instinctual renunciation which
is the source of civilization. In the last analysis, the individual is "the enemy of culture," for culture demands
that he renounce his individual search for instinctual gratification, and place the energies of the instincts in the service of the "higher," *aim-inhibited* goals of civilization. The
individual grudgingly renounces the Pleasure Principle, but
this renunciation is never entirely successful. The repressed
instincts remain the source of neurotic suffering and of
anti-social acts which ultimately threaten the very existence
of civilization, defending it against the assaults of its un-
willing, adherents. Individuals are reconciled, at least temporarily, to the restrictions and renunciations required of
them by civilization, by the promise of a better life to come
and by the religious sanctions (taboos) which declare the
social and moral order to be God-ordained.

Freud argues that the ancient struggle between religion and science as to which more accurately describes the nature of reality must be decided in favor of science. What status in the psychic economy can then be assigned to the complicated interweaving of ideas, hopes, wishes, theories and judgments which we call religion? WHAT IS RELIGION?

Freud was an uncompromising realist. He sought to live as entirely free of self-delusion as is possible in human life. The goal of Psychoanalysis in particular, as the most comprehensive scientific psychology, was the goal of science in general, what Freud terms the "Scientific Weltanschauung," the scientific world-view. A fuller discussion of this assertion occurs below. For the moment we may define the Scientific Weltanschauung as that philosophy whose search for truth is guided solely by objectively verifiable, empirical, experimental evidence; the philosophy which seeks a lawful, natural explanation for all phenomena; the philosophy which takes observation and experience as the sole criterion in determining matters of truth and falsehood.

Freud here describes Psychoanalysis as a tool of scientific research "as objetive as the infinitesimal calculus." The purpose of *The Future of an Illusion* is to subject religious phenomena to psychoanalytic scientific investigation. In so doing, we are returned once again to the infantile unconscious mental life of humanity and its primary mechanisms, wish-fulfillments.

Illusion and Delusion

In distinguishing the concept of "illusion," from that of "delusion," Freud suggests that religion is not necessarily in error about the nature of reality. A *delusion* is just such an error. An *illusion* on the other hand is the manifestation of unconscious wishes. Its structure represents the projected fulfillment of infantile needs. Hence, religion as an *illusion* can be viewed as an accurate representation of reality, if

we realize that it is unconscious PSYCHOLOGICAL RE-
ALITY *NOT* OBJECTIVE REALITY to which religion
gives complete expression. But it is necessary to note that
religion claims to describe objective ontological reality in its
entirety MORE ACCURATELY than does physical science.
Therein lies the true source of the ancient conflict between
science and religion. Of course, Freud resolves this debate
in favor of the Scientific Weltanschauung; in fact, he seems
almost to be issuing a typical Freudian "disclaimer," by asserting that religion is not completely in error concerning
the nature of reality. From a scientific psychoanalytic point
of view, religion is most certainly wrong in claiming to have
discovered *anything* about reality which comes into conflict
with what physical science discovers. Religion is also unaware of the fact that the reality with which it is dealing
presents what Freud described in *Totem and Taboo* as "a
complete overevaluation of psychic reality at the expense of
physical reality." Why then the Freudian "disclaimer," that
is, the proposition that religious *illusion* differs in kind
from psychotic *delusion,* and religion may not be entirely
in error?

Freud's "Disclaimers"

It is significant that in his two other major works on the
theory of religion, *Totem and Taboo* and *Moses and Monotheism,* Freud issued quite similar "disclaimers" to the one
found here in *The Future of an Illusion.* Put simply and
briefly, in all three works Freud first denies that he is
seeking to destroy the objective validity of religious traditions, customs, theologies and beliefs, and then proceeds to
destroy them. At the beginning of the fourth essay in
Totem and Taboo, "The Return of Totemism in Childhood,"
Freud writes that the Primal Horde theory may not be the
most valid or important source for an understanding of
religion. As we have seen above, he then proceeds to de-
molish the superstructure of not only primitive religions,
but of Christianity and Judaism as well, laying bare their

foundations in the SAME HISTORICAL EVENT, the murder of the primal father! It is patently clear that Freud considers his theory as THE explanation of the paraphernalia of all religions. The "disclaimer" is somewhat modified in *Moses and Monotheism,* and does not strike the reader as quite so contradictory in comparison to what Freud has said and done in *Totem and Taboo.* In the first paragraph of his last book Freud does recognize that what he is doing is not "a deed to be undertaken light-heartedly," that is, the denial of Moses' Jewishness with all of its implications for the Judeo-Christian tradition, and especially "by one belonging to that people." He then proceeds to do just that!

The assertion in *The Future of an Illusion* that religion is not necessarily in error about reality is followed by a convincing set of arguments which psychoanalytically demonstrate that religion is indeed TOTALLY IN ERROR ABOUT WHAT IT TAKES TO BE THE NATURE OF THE REAL WORLD. ONLY SCIENCE IS NOT ILLUSION. "But it would be an illusion to suppose that we could get anywhere else what it cannot give us." This very last sentence of the work clearly asserts that religion must surrender to the scientific world-view, and that when its theories of reality, both external in the form of a theory of the physical world, and internal, in the form of a theory of human nature, conflict with the Scientific Weltanschauung (and in the case of a theory of human nature, with the Psychoanalytic Weltanschauung), then it is religious *illusion* that must give way before scientific truth.

What reason can we find to explain these Freudian "disclaimers"? The answer Freud gave most explicitly in June 1938 in beginning to write the second part of the Moses book. He had recently arrived in London after fleeing the Nazi invasion of Austria. In the atmosphere of political freedom which he found in England, Freud wrote that his intention NOT TO PUBLISH the Moses book, which he never deleted from the first part of this essay written in Austria before June 1938, was caused by his fear of conflict with the powerful Catholic, government-supported censorship in his native land. Freud's stated intention to withhold his last book from publication, had he remained in Austria, was caused by his fear of losing the protection of the Catholic church, not for himself personally, but for the practice of Psychoanalysis. It was quite conceivable to Freud, in the political atmosphere of Austria in 1938, that the publication of the Moses book, striking at the heart of Christianity as well as Judaism, would have brought on the banning of the practice of Psychoanalysis, and the further publication and distribution of psychoanalytic books and periodicals. Without question, this fact also explains the earlier "disclaimers" which are found in *Totem* and *Future*.

Dynamics of Religion

What then is Freud's final evaluation of the essence and validity of human religions? The modicum of truth contained with religious traditions is that they preserve historical memories in severely distorted form, the memories of the Primal Horde experience. But these memories are so distorted and disguised that they fail to render an accurate account of the genesis of religion. They are accurate in symbolic form, but totally wrong in literal content.

The contents of religion represent the projection of unconscious infantile needs and wishes onto the external world. As in the psychology of mass politics, these infantile needs express dependence upon the father. The psychology of religion in no way differs from the psychology of politics. It is a collective projection of unconscious infantile anxiety and dependence. The same dynamics are in operation in mystical, religious and political behavior. The great Russian novelist Fydor Dostoyevsky, whom Freud much admired, wrote that the overwhelming majority of men require *Mystery*, *Miracle* and *Authority* to enable them to tolerate life. In both religion and politics Freud most certainly agreed, and although he was well aware of the vital part unconscious wishes and needs play in human psychol-

THE INTERPRETATION OF DREAMS 113

ogy, the prime goal of Psychoanalysis always remained the overcoming of the infantile mental life and a re-education to reality. The Scientific Weltanschauung and the Primacy of the Intellect, the two cornerstones of Psychoanalysis as a philosophy of life, enable human beings to live without illusions and to relinquish them in all of their institutionalized forms.

Is Psychoanalysis a Science?

Freud never wavered in his conviction that Psychoanalysis was a true science of the human mind, indeed, THE true science of the human mind in all its ramifications. The goal of the Psychoanalytic Weltanschauung was "...to range the neuroses and psychoses among the sciences by means of the theory of repression and wish-fulfillment." This project for a scientific psychology has been hotly disputed and a number of specific objections raised:

1. The unconscious cannot be directly observed.
2. Freud's interpretations were arbitrary and made to conform to a pre-established scheme.
3. There exist numerous other psychologies which can present evidence for their priority over Psychoanalysis as the definitive science of the mind. Psychoanalysis can claim no higher incidence of "cures" in therapy than other therapies.
4. Subjectivism: The analyst projects his own feelings and ideas onto the patient's behavior. He "looks for" specific interpretations consonant with his own theories.
5. The predictive value of Psychoanalysis is erratic and no greater than any other explanation of human behavior.
6. Freud did not emphasize the importance of social conditioning. He was totally committed to the evolutionary-biological standpoint.
7. There is too much sexual emphasis in Psychoanalysis. Other forces of equal or greater importance exist in determining the human personality.

8. Freud was limited by the time and place in which he lived. His discoveries are "relative," not "universal."

9. Instead of science, Freud had founded a new "religion" to replace those he had swept away. He was dictatorial, authoritative, dogmatic and vindictive toward his followers who disagreed with him.

10. Freud's propensity for revision and correction leaves the student unsure as to the exact doctrines of Psychoanalysis. Which works are to be held as canonical, those of the *Clinical Period* (1895-1917) or those works of the *Metapsychological Period* which appear after the discovery of the Death Instinct in 1920?

11. What accounts for the hostile reactions to his new "science"? Why has Psychoanalysis received relatively limited acceptance by both the medical and academic professions?

Freud's biographer Ernest Jones has written that Psychoanalysis can never attain to mathematical certainty, and that was never Freud's intention in describing it as a science. As we have noted, Freud was fond of drawing comparisons to Psychoanalysis from ancient languages, and as Jones notes, a high degree of probability has been achieved in the reading of ancient inscriptions. Certainly Psychoanalysis can be included within Aristotle's well-known dictum, concerning ethical sciences, that we are not to expect greater certainty from a given subject matter than it is capable of providing. But this lack of absolute certainty in no way prevented Aristotle from including the subject matter of human behavior within the purview of "practical" science.

Psychoanalysis and Scientific Method

Freud repeatedly argued that his discoveries had in no way been influenced by any preconceived theory; in fact, he took technical philosophers to task for what was to him the gravest intellectual sin imaginable, making facts fit some *a priori* notion of what reality ought to be, instead of investigating it as it is. Freud was at least as surprised as his contemporaries by the nature of his discoveries. His credo was to look at the facts until they spoke to him. This emphasis on PERCEPTION and OBSERVATION as the basic tools of psychoanalytic investigation entitled it to be included among all sciences which anyway begin in empiricism. But the activity of psychoanalytic observation must first and foremost be "learned on oneself." It will be recalled that the cornerstone of Psychoanalysis, *The Interpretation of Dreams,* Freud's first and in many ways greatest discovery, was made through the analysis of his own dreams. Freud felt any good dreamer, in the sense of a prolific dreamer, could carry out the same process on his own dreams. The necessity for self-observation as the starting point of psychoanalytic theory lends superficial credence to criticisms *2* and *4* above, that Psychoanalysis is arbitrary in its interpretations as well as subjective, deriving solely from the private, relative experience of the individual. The inference followed that Freud had projected his own severe Oedipus Complex onto his patients, thus discovering what he put there. These criticisms presuppose that it is never possible to be objective in the process of self-understanding. If true, then all psychologies and all theories of human nature are subjective projections of their authors or discoverers and the possibility of knowledge of human nature is reduced to solipsism. If, on the other hand, objective knowledge of human nature is possible, then some other criterion must be produced to specify in just what manner Freud is to be accused of projecting his own psychology onto others, while other theories of personality are exempted from the same accusation.

Criticism *No. 5* merely highlights the fact that every good analyst knows that he is limited in his knowledge and fallible in his judgments. The variable factors in each individual case in therapy are potentially so complex, that the therapist's capacity to "predict" the outcome of therapy is severely circumscribed. The fact of limited predictability holds true for even the more exact sciences. There is much that is unknown in any given stage of scientific development, much that is guessed at, and many crucial errors made on the way to shaping a scientific theory, much less a scientific law. The tentative nature of all conclusions in science is about the only absolute statement we can make. This would suggest an answer to criticism *No. 10,* that Freud shifted his basic positions on the elements of human psychology a number of times during his lifetime. There is NO FINAL AND CANONICAL set of doctrines which make of Psychoanalysis a new religion (criticism *No. 9*). FREUD DID NOT KNOW EVERYTHING. PSYCHOANALYSIS DOES NOT POSSESS ALL THE ANSWERS TO THE PROBLEMS OF HUMAN NATURE. NO SCIENCE HAS YET ACHIEVED PERFECTION.

Experimental Limitations

A real limitation occurs in Psychoanalysis which differentiates it from physical science proper. That is the fact of the absence of strict *experimental* verification; patients cannot be dealt with experimentally in the manner of physical particles or lower forms of life. The experimental factor has led to a much higher degree of predictability though by no means "certainty," in the physical sciences. Yet even in these sciences hypotheses are advanced which escape direct experimental verification and yet are accepted as more or less valid explanations of obscure problems. Astronomers, for example, are still occupied with trying to solve the problem of the origin of the physical universe. Their deductions and theories IN NO WAY DIFFER from Freud's procedures concerning the origins of human culture. Evidence is gathered from a wide range of sources and then a general theory is propounded in an attempt to relate and best explain the nature of the evidence. But, NO EXPERIMENTAL PROOF is possible in dealing with past and unique events, the origins of the physical universe or the origins of human civilizations.

From this it follows that criticism *No. 1*, that the human unconscious mind is unobservable, is juvenile. NO LAW OF SCIENCE IS DIRECTLY OBSERVABLE. One cannot inspect the LAW of Gravity or the LAWS of Evolution, only particular instances of them. Freud argued that one can more accurately relate and explain the multiplicity of instances of human behavior by the deductive assumption of the existence of unconscious mental processes than by any available alternative explanation. Physics explains seemingly unrelated events, the fall of an apple toward the earth, the fall of a coin, and the "fall" of the moon, by deducing the existence of the Law of Gravity. But the Law of Gravity is NEVER observed, only its manifestation in isolated instances. But the conviction of the existence of a law explaining these instances is the essence of the scientific mentality. The Law of the Primary Process functions in exactly the same manner in psychoanalytic science. The existence of the unconscious relates and explains an enormous variety of apparently unrelated behavioral manifestations, slips of the tongue, dreaming, neurotic symptoms, psychosis, perversions, the nature of art, religion and morality, by a single unifying principle.

Freud clearly affirmed the possibility of differing specific interpretations of evidence in Psychoanalysis, but the elimination of alternative possibilities is one of science's greatest achievements. Criticism *No. 3* raises the issue of why Psychoanalysis fails to bring conviction to many students of human behavior. Why are there so many alternatives to the psychoanalytic theory? After all, we possess a severely limited number of possible alternatives in physical theory, for instance in physics, the wave theory of the transmission of light vs. the particle theory. (A. N. Whitehead has suggested a third possibility, the "wavicle" theory.) Still, this is a modest number of alternatives compared to the literally dozens of psychologies, psychotherapies and theories of human nature competing with Psychoanalysis as THE explanation of homo sapiens' mentality. This criticism is certainly the most cogent of those listed above and Freud never really answered it. It is perhaps unanswerable. Suffice it to say that Freud felt he had amassed a convincing amount of evidence in favor of Psychoanalysis, and he expressed the hope, in *The Future of an Illusion,* that reason would prevail in the end, and Psychoanalysis would be judged superior to its opponents.

After reading the present work, the student will be able to evaluate criticism *No. 6* that Freud did not place sufficient emphasis on social factors. THE WHOLE DYNAMICS OF MENTAL FUNCTIONING IN PSYCHO-ANALYSIS IS DETERMINED BY THE INTERACTION OF *THE INDIVIDUAL AND SOCIETY.* As for criticism *No. 7,* Freud never denied that other factors beside sexuality play a vital role in understanding human behavior. Hunger, thirst, man's lengthy dependence in infancy, aggression, natural curiosity, plus the so-called higher elements in human nature all contribute to this understanding. It was simply because human sexuality had been subjected to restrictions that no other human instinct had, and its importance as *a* central feature in human experience (not *THE* central feature) had been so long denied, that Freud's discoveries concerning the nature and function of sexuality came as such a shock to mankind.

In dealing with criticism *No. 8,* we may affirm that Freud was no more limited and determined by the relativity of his time and place than were Homer in ancient Greece, Michelangelo in sixteenth-century Italy, Jesus in first-century Judea, Archimedes in third-century Syracuse, or Einstein in twentieth-century Europe. If Freud's discoveries are valid, then they are valid for all men in all times and all places. Simply because the late twentieth century is a time of universal cultural and ethical relativism does not mean that it holds a sounder or more accurate view of the human condition than the epochs preceding it which asserted the universality of human values. This is certainly no philosophical refutation of the doctrines of cultural relativism. It is simply meant to point out to the student that because a set of ideas is current, contemporary, widely-accepted and popular, in no way signifies that these ideas are right.

Freud did not found a new religion (criticism *No. 9*) and, according to many who worked with him throughout his lifetime (E. Jones, T. Reik, W. Reich, and many others) he was the very antithesis of a new Messiah. The student of Freud continually marvels at his open-mindedness. One thing the founder of a new religion must never do is either ADMIT HE WAS IN ERROR, CHANGE HIS MIND, or PROPOSE A NEW IDEA AS TENTATIVE AND UN-CERTAIN. Freud, of course, did all three and on more than one occasion. Psychoanalysis began when Freud recognized his error in taking Hysterics at their word and not at first recognizing the nature of Screen-Memories. He certainly changed his mind on the theory of instincts, and the theory of the Death Instinct, for all its importance in later Freud-ian theory, is put forth as a highly speculative idea. Freud was emphatically no Messiah. One further comment on the tentative nature of much of Freud's work and the shifting positions he took on many basic issues in human psychology. All great creative thinkers undergo a lengthy process of development, especially if their creative life spans half a century as Freud's did. The most seminal philosopher in the history of Western thought, Plato, severely modified many of his basic doctrines, and constantly questioned his convictions from varying and conflicting viewpoints. The Plato who wrote the mystical *Phaedo* at the age of 26 is not the Plato who wrote the pedestrian *Laws* at the age of 80. Beethoven's *First Symphony* is separated from his *Ninth Symphony* by an almost incredible life of spiritual growth and development. And the Freud who authored *Studies in Hysteria* is not the same Freud of *The Interpretation of Dreams, Three Essays on the Theory of Sexuality, Totem and Taboo* or *Beyond the Pleasure Principle*. Freud never said the final word on what he recognized to be the most complex and mysterious of all human phenomena, the Unconscious.

Criticism *No. 11* listed above, concerning the lack of acceptance by the medical and academic professions of much of Freud's work, has been in part already answered in our discussion of the concept of Resistance to anxiety-producing truths. A number of instances of the first reactions to Freud's publications will be discussed later.

"Civilization and Its Discontents" (1930)

Freud's last Metapsychological essay, *Civilization and Its Discontents*, may in time stand as his most unique contribution to the theory of civilization. It represents the inclusion of the Death Instinct within the context of the collective manifestations of human psychology rather than its ramifications in the behavior of the individual alone. The principal derivative of the Death Instinct, the instinct for aggression, poses the most potent threat to the continued existence of civilized institutions, and Freud is deeply skeptical concerning the eventual outcome of the struggle between the repressive, aim-inhibited, sublimative forces of civilization on the one hand, and the powerful thrust of the Death Instinct on the other.

We have seen Freud's discussion of the inevitable conflict produced in each individual by the demands of his instinctual apparatus as it seeks to meet the repressive requirements of civilization. This conflict is invariably resolved in favor of civilization at the expense of human happiness. Freud gives us one of the simplest and most direct definitions of human happiness in the history of moral speculation. HAPPINESS IS TOTAL INSTINCTUAL GRATIFICATION. And it is *impossible!* Much of the instinctual energy that would be devoted to the pursuit of the individual's personal satisfaction must be employed in the service of civilization, especially in the civilized requirements to work and to postpone sexual gratification far beyond the time of biological readiness.

But the Pleasure Principle which dominates the Primary Process never completely surrenders its privileged place in the mental economy. From this bedrock fact, two important consequences follow. *First:* Civilization is required to replace individual satisfactions in order to compensate in some small measure for the instinctual renunciations it binds in its own service. And, *Second:* A new realm of psychic functioning "splits off" from the rest of the personality and develops into the activity of fantasy in which the Pleasure Principle maintains its supremacy.

Purpose of Civilization

In creating *Substitute Gratifications,* civilization compensates the individual by redirecting his libidinal energies into socially acceptable forms of amusement and diversion. But as the name implies, these activities are substitutes for the real thing, instinctual gratification. Sexual gratification is the prototype of all forms of individual happiness but it is anti-social; that is, sexual happiness does not serve the requirements of civilization and in fact may deter the sexually happy individual from surrendering his libidinal energies to compulsive labor and the postponement of gratification until the socially approved moment. The purpose of civilization then becomes the constant attempt to divert the individual from private sexual gratification into collective, socially productive and acceptable activities. In order that civilized life may not be totally intolerable, civilization creates the Substitute Gratifications which replace sexual happiness as the goal of the Pleasure Principle. Freud lists alcohol, drugs and tobacco as physical substitutes; art, religion, politics and in many ways science too, as intellectual replacements for the lost sexual happiness.

Paradox of Human Sexuality

Still Freud raises the question, knowing that the satisfaction of the sexual instinct provides mankind its most intense pleasures and deepest happines, why would men ever turn from this path to follow the path of second-best, Substitute Gratifications? Here we come upon the greatest paradox of man's sexual life, and an explanation of why so many human beings reject sexual love as the source of ultimate happiness, resigning themselves to substitutes and fantasy. Freud writes, "We are never so defenseless as when we are in love." The source of our greatest happiness is at the same time the source of our greatest misery. In the state of being in love (and for Freud, all forms of love are derivatives of sensual love and in many cases substitutes for it), the Ego loses one of its principal abilities, the capacity to distinguish physical from psychical reality. Its boundaries "dissolve" and the major function of defending the psyche against psychological pain is paralyzed. Freud could find only two comparable states of mental functioning (or dysfunctioning!), the state of being hypnotized, and psychosis! The individual in love has no more ability to test reality or defend himself against pain (the two primary functions of the Ego) than does a person in a hypnotic trance or suffering from a psychosis. This is the reason why the path of sexual happiness is renounced by so many human beings. The Ego is defenseless, susceptible to severe pain, and incapable of distinguishing reality from its wishes. The object of sexual love is invariably "over-estimated" as to its real nature. But since sexual love IS happiness, yet becomes impossible in civilization, happiness therefore becomes impossible. Freud advises that men parcel out their libidinal energies in a controlled and rational fashion and seek in creative work, especially art and scientific investigation, a surer though infinitely less intense source of happiness. In the end, Substitute Gratifications become the only guarantee against the hypnotic-psychotic defenselessness of sexual love.

The renunciations and repressions brought on by the threatened loss of love in childhood produce the prototype of all adult libidinal resignation. The threat of the loss of the parent's love coupled with the defenseless state of the infant's Ego initiates the process of civilizing him, that is enabling him to tolerate greater and greater instinctual renunciations, even at the cost of eventual neurotic illness or just plain ordinary unhappiness. (Thoreau: "The mass of men lead lives of quiet desperation.")

But as cited above, a second consequence results from the refusal of the Pleasure Principle to totally submit to the demands of civilization. An independent kingdom is set up within the boundaries of the psyche, free of the repressive strictures of the Reality Principle and ruled by the indestructible urge toward pleasure. This is the realm of fantasy and imagination. It also includes the previously discussed realm of the sexual perversions in which the infantile mental life survives into adulthood and continues to defy the demands of the Reality Principle, although paying the price of a distorted sex life.

Consequences of the Conflict

The products of the imagination, great works of art, were for Freud the most completely satisfactory Substitute Gratifications, and their essence will be shortly examined. But a final somber footnote was added by Freud to his conviction that sexuality was not the path to human happiness. He speculated that the sexual life of civilized man might be involved in a process of biological involution; that is, on the way to becoming a rudimentary function just as hair and little toes are becoming rudimentary organs, no longer necessary, hence, in the process of being discarded by the evolutionary law of Natural Selection. Certainly, Freud opines, the sexual life of civilized man, as compared to the sexual lives of ancient and primitive men, is "severely impaired," and his capacity for sensual enjoyment markedly diminished. Perhaps, in addition to the severe wounds inflicted on civilized man's sexuality by his repressive institutions, there exists "...something in the nature of the function itself" that inhibits the pleasure premium placed by his libido on sexual gratification. This Freudian opinion possesses momentous consequences for the fate of man and civilization far beyond the sorrowful fact of the passing of the human animal's most intensely pleasurable activity.

We may recall from Freud's discussion in *Group Psychology and the Analysis of the Ego* that it is the cohesive force of Eros alone that binds men together in communities larger than the family unit, and that the energy of Eros is a sublimated form of libido, sexual energy. It is Eros the sublimated derivative of libidinal sexuality, that performs an even more essential function in relation to the Death Instinct.

In his final explanation of the Dialectic of History, Freud viewed history as a gigantic battleground for the forces of Eros and the Death Instinct. What had first been viewed as the arena in which the individual's instinctual demands struggled against the repressive forces of civilization and subsequently, as the human races struggle against the inherited unconscious memories of the will of the Primal Father locked in conflict with the desire for sexual freedom and happiness, attains to almost cosmic dimensions in *Civilization and Its Discontents* as Freud reverts to mytho-poetic language to describe the dialectical conflict between Eros and the Death Instinct.

Eros-Death Instinct Dialectic

It will be remembered that the Death Instinct, the organic search for final homogeneity and release from all biological tensions, becomes the primary drive in the human organism, more fundamental than the life instinct, Eros. The wish to die is only temporarily diverted from its pre-ordained goal by the energies of Eros. Eros *binds* the Death Instinct and leads it outward from the organism in the form of aggression against the external world, especially sublimated, constructive aggression as in the case of overcoming natural obstacles in the process of building canals, railroads, bridges and cities. But as mentioned above, the cohesive force of Eros and its essential function of deflecting the Death Instinct into the external world in the form of socially valuable acts begins to weaken as the basic energy of the sexual libido is repressed and the biological function of involution occurs. Groups, communities, national states lose their cohesiveness. The dissipation of Eros (through the continuing repression of libidinal energies) destroys social groups which constitute the nucleus of civilization. As Eros is weakened through the repression of libido, the *destructive* aspects of the Death Instinct press to the fore until an almost "pure culture of the Death Instinct" appears. The crazy dialectic moves on impersonally and inevitably. Civilization derives its cohesive energies from Eros. Eros is the sublimated form of Libido; Libido must be repressed and its energies diverted to the requirements of the Reality Principle. But in repressing the Libido, civilization is at the same time weakening the forces of Eros which hold it together! As the forces of Eros weaken, the Death Instinct begins to permeate all the activities and institutions of civilization, threatening its very survival. Thus, the last immense paradox of the Freudian theory of civilization strikes home with telling force.

THE VERY ENERGIES BY WHICH CIVILIZATION SURVIVES AND PERPETUATES ITSELF, EROS, ARE PRODUCED BY THE REPRESSION OF THE SOURCES OF THOSE ENERGIES, LIBIDO. THE REPRESSION OF LIBIDO UPON WHICH CIVILIZATION DEPENDS FOR ITS SURVIVAL, WEAKENS EROS WHOSE MAJOR FUNCTION OF BINDING THE DEATH INSTINCT IN THE SERVICE OF CIVILIZATION CAN NO LONGER BE EFFECTIVELY CARRIED OUT. THE LIBERATION OF THE DEATH INSTINCT DUE TO THE WEAKENING OF EROS DUE TO THE REPRESSION OF LIBIDO UPON WHICH CIVILIZATION DEPENDS FOR ITS EXISTENCE THEN BECOMES THE SINGLE GREATEST THREAT TO THE CONTINUED SURVIVAL AND PERPETUATION OF CIVILIZATION!

Freud's ultimate deductions in Metapsychology place the human race and all its institutions in an inescapable double-bind!

Freud would not "offer consolation" to his fellow men. His last words on the fate of civilization echo the pessimistic and ambivalent mood which increased in strength as Freud's life progressed. We might fancifully suggest that the "pure culture of the Death Instinct" had begun to possess Freud himself! After stating that he could listen with sympathy to anyone who claimed that the whole business of creating culture at the expense of human happiness was not worth the trouble, Freud concluded *Civilization and Its Discontents* with a typical provocative peroration: "And now it is to be expected that the other of the two 'Heavenly Powers,' external Eros, will make an effort to assert himself in the struggle with his equally immortal adversary. But who can foresee with what success and with what result?"

PART FOUR

THE ANATOMY OF THE MENTAL PERSONALITY

Freud described the division of mental acts into Conscious and Unconscious as "the fundamental premises of psychoanalysis." But he never sought systematically to dissect and label the various meanings given to mental processes until the writing of *The Ego and the Id* in 1923. This section of our study guide will deal with Freud's mature formulation of the nature and function of the various parts of the mental personality. Much of our previous discussion has dealt with these mental realms and activities as they apply directly to an understanding of dreams, neuroses, etc. Now we shall discuss them as they relate to EACH OTHER, as well as what they are in themselves.

Although Freud considered the discovery of unconscious mental activity to be his finest achievement, and although most of the pivotal writings in the pioneer years of Psychoanalysis deal with the nature and function of the Primary Process, after 1920 Freud shifted his focus to a study of the nature of the Ego. This shift in emphasis brought about new discoveries concerning both the conscious and unconscious realms, clarified earlier ambiguities, and structured the theory of the mental personality along more clearly defined parameters.

Ego, Id and Super-Ego

A definitive terminology to describe and distinguish the various realms of mental functioning begins with the adoption of the term ID. Freud borrowed this term from the analyst George Groddeck who had gotten it from the philosopher Friedrich Nietzsche. *Id means It* (in German, Das Es), and Freud attaches this term to ALL UNCONSCIOUS MENTAL PROCESSES WHICH CANNOT BE MADE CONSCIOUS. The Id is the source of the instincts. The Id is the "Kingdom of the Illogical." It is the least organized realm of mental personality. In the essay, *The Unconscious* (1915), Freud had begun to delineate just exactly "what" the Unconscious contained, "where" it was located, and "how" it acted. By 1923 he was able to present his most complete theory of the essence of unconscious mental actions and provide some sharp revision of his earlier theories of their relation to consciousness. The mental apparatus is divided into three analytically distinct though functionally intertwined systems: *Consciousness* (Cs.), the *Unconscious* (Ucs.), and the *Pre-Conscious* (Pcs). In addition, he distinguishes three realms of the mind WHICH ARE NOT IDENTICAL with the three systems just now defined. These three realms are the *Ego*, the *Id*, and the *Super-Ego*. Finally, Freud outlined what he referred to as three methods of approaching a study of the mental personality, the *topographical, the dynamic*, and the *economic*. This vocabulary gives us Freud's most complete theoretical statement on the nature of the human mind.

The evolution of the theory of the mental personality over a quarter century from the time of Breuer's discovery of the *conscience seconde* to his own formulations in the mid-1920's led Freud to this general set of conclusions:

1. The Ego is identical with the activities of consciousness. Its prime function is to test reality and signal danger to the organism when anxiety appears. BUT NOT THE WHOLE OF THE EGO IS CONSCIOUS. Part of the Ego is Pre-Conscious, facing toward the Unconscious so

to speak, rather than toward the external world. It is the pre-conscious part of the Ego that is the source of the Dream Censorship. But part of the Ego is also Unconscious. IT IS THE UNCONSCIOUS PART OF THE EGO THAT IS REPRESSED. Repression occurs in the Ego AGAINST ITSELF! The activities of censorship and repression thus become ego-functions. *Unconsciousness is no longer a quality associated with the Id alone.* The Id cannot be made conscious. But the repressed portion of the Ego can and must be if repressions are to be lifted.

2. The Ego, however, grows out of the Id. The Id remains under the sway of the Pleasure Principle. The Ego, however, is severely modified by the Reality Principle. The Ego must mediate between the clamorous demands of the Id for instinctual gratification and the threatening dangers of the external world.

3. Topographically (we might almost say "geographically"), the Ego is located at the periphery of the organism, at the surface of the body; perhaps, at the cortex of the brain. The Ego is first and foremost a "bodily" ego. It controls the accesses to motility and represents what we term reason.

4. Dynamically (meaning the performance of some energetic function in the mental apparatus) the EGO IS THE SOURCE OF REPRESSION. Repression is directed against the instincts of the Id which the Ego, in its Pre-Conscious condition, considers threatening. The danger signal which activates the function of Repression in the Ego is Anxiety. This Anxiety is associated with the forbidden impulses of childhood. Anxiety (now internalized) threatens the Ego, as fear of parental punishment (external prohibitions) once did. Freud here presents an important modification of his original theory of Anxiety. *Repression does not cause Anxiety. Anxiety is the cause of Repression!* Repression results in a portion of the Ego being cut-off from conscious contact with the rest of the

Ego. It is this repressed portion of the Ego which maintains contact with the unconscious Id, BUT IS NOT THE SAME AS THE ID.

5. The third mental agency, the Super-Ego, is in part conscious in the form of the Ego-Ideal (discussed above) or conscience, and in part unconscious. It is the unconscious portion of the Super-Ego which is in intimate contact with the Id, which the conscious part of the Ego is not. The Super-Ego oversees the relationship between the repressed part of the Ego (the forbidden childhood wishes) and the unconscious Id, which is the dynamic source of the instinctual energies which support the repressed wishes and thoughts in the Ego. It punishes the conscious Ego by producing a strong sense of guilt, not for what the Ego consciously performs, but rather for those forbidden impulses which the unconscious-repressed portion of the Ego wishes to obey. Guilt, however may be both conscious and unconscious; that is the conscious Ego may not be aware that its actions and judgments are caused by unconscious guilt emanating from the Super-Ego. The Super-Ego represents the introjection of parental demands on the child, as well as parental attitudes toward sex, aggression, etc. It is the heir to the Oedipus Complex; that is, it perpetuates (unconsciously) those attitudes towards the instincts which the parents made evident to the child at the oedipal stage of his psychosexual development. In childhood, the instincts were actually frustrated by the parents. Anxiety was produced in the child which brought about the repression of these instincts and the renunciation of the Oedipus Complex. The instinct for aggression, which the child would like to have directed against a frustrating reality, is bound by the Super-Ego, and directed back against the Ego in the form of self-reproaches, condemnation, and a sense of guilt. However, the intensity of guilt-feelings is not contingent alone upon the intensity of the parents' frustrations. A constitutional factor en-

ters here; that is, just how powerful the aggressive instincts may be in a given individual. The more powerful the unconscious desire to aggress, the more intense the feelings of guilt produced in the Ego (both conscious and unconscious). The punitive agency of the Super-Ego is for the most part unconscious, in contrast to the Ego-Ideal which is identified with moral conscience and is of course, conscious. The Super-Ego is not "realistic"; that is, it does not represent the requirements of present psychological reality, but the demands made upon the individual in the past. Its attitude Freud describes as "totally un-psychological," and a major task of therapy is to seek to alleviate the irrational, infantile sense of guilt caused by the Super-Ego. It is the conscious Ego which is most in touch with the requirements of present reality, while the Id represents "the demands of the organic past," that is, man's evolutionary, biological, instinctual heritage. The mediating Ego is often caught between the imperious demands of the instincts, the objective obstacles and threats which civilization presents to the gratification of those instincts, and the irrational demands of the Super-Ego for instinctual renunciation. No wonder, Freud remarked, the Ego so seldom succeeds in achieving a satisfactory solution to the problems generated by the conflicting demands of these opposing forces, and breaks down and becomes neurotic.

Topographical, Dynamic and Economic Aspects of the Mental Anatomy

1. By *Topographical*, Freud means the physical location of the three mental agencies. As we have said the Ego lies toward the periphery of the body and is in contact with the world. The Id is what Freud describes as the somatic source of all mental states, the biological instincts which find psychological representation in the Ego's consciousness. The Super-Ego in the form of the Ego-Ideal is actually a portion of the conscious Ego, but is for the

most part in closer contact with the Id. It can employ the unconscious instincts for aggression in the Id, as well as the repressed aggressions of the Ego, to punish the Ego. BUT IT IS EXTREMELY DIFFICULT TO DETERMINE THE TOPOGRAPHY OF THE SUPER-EGO, except to note that it is like the Ego, a modification of the Id, though unlike the Ego, it remains unconscious.

2. *Dynamically* (functionally) speaking, there is only ONE UNCONSCIOUS mental agency, the Id. The Pre-Conscious and repressed portions of the Ego are capable of being made conscious. But the Id is not. Freud writes, "...in a descriptive sense there are two kinds of Unconscious but in a dynamic sense just one."

3. By the term *Economic*, Freud meant to describe in just what way the individual's instinctual energies are divided up and parceled out to the various mental agencies, how much is conscious and how much unconscious, how much repressed and bound in neurotic symptoms, how much available to the Ego for normal external discharge, how much retained by the Super-Ego to be used against the Ego, and how much discharged in a guilt-free fashion.

The Anatomy of Mental Personality is perhaps the most difficult and obscure of all Freud's theories, and he was well aware of it. In the *Outline of Psychoanalysis* (1939) Freud confessed that of the true meaning of the mental quality he called unconscious, as well as the true meaning of the mental quality he called pre-conscious, as well as the distinctions between them, *HE KNEW NOTHING!* Freud's words on these most difficult problems should comfort the student wrestling with an attempt to comprehend the vistas of human psychology opening before him. "...here we have approached the still shrouded secret of the nature of what is mental...and the profound obscurity of our ignorance is scarcely illuminated by a glimmer or two of light."

PART FIVE

THE FREUDIAN THEORY OF ART

1. "The Relation of the Poet to Daydreaming" (1908)
2. *Jokes and Their Relation to the Unconscious* (1905)
3. *Leonardo da Vinci: A Study in Psychosexuality* (1910)

Freud considered art to be the most important substitute gratification that civilization offered men in exchange for the repression of their instinctual life, and his writings are laced through and through with a sense of wonder at the achievements of the great literary and pictorial artists of the Western tradition. (Freud tended to "distrust" the effect of great music since he was unable to find an intellectual explanation for it.) Freud credited creative writers, and not always first-rate authors, with anticipating many of the discoveries of Psychoanalysis which had come to them in flashes of inspiration while he was fated to laboriously struggle to put together the evidence in pedestrian scientific fashion. One of Freud's proudest achievements was the winning of the Goethe Prize for Literature, and the book of his of which he was most personally fond was *Leonardo da Vinci: A Study in Psychosexuality*.

As early in his career as the writing of the *Interpretation of Dreams*, Freud indicated that the insights of Psychoanalysis could prove a fresh approach to the major classics of Western literature. He suggested that the riddle of Shakespeare's *Hamlet* could be divined by linking it to the *Oedipus Rex* of Sophocles, and in a letter to a friend written in 1897 Freud outlined the psychoanalytic solution. Hamlet's behavior could only be understood in terms of his neurotic inhibitions. While the term "Oedipus Complex" does not appear in Freud's writings until 1910, Hamlet was certanly suffering from the same condition as King Oedipus in the Greek tragedy. The difference lay in the fact that Oedipus had actually killed his father and married his mother while Prince Hamlet was paralyzed and prevented from acting because of his UNCONSCIOUS WISH TO COMMIT THESE UNIVERSALLY FORBIDDEN ACTS.

Preliminary Approaches: "The Relation of the Poet to Daydreaming" (1908)

In 1908 Freud wrote a short paper entitled "The Relation of the Poet to Daydreaming" in which he argued that the secret of the artist's power over his audience was the ability to disguise and then portray the forbidden themes which all men have repressed into their unconscious. The artist supplies his audience with a high premium of pleasure by allowing it to enjoy in fantasy the unconscious wishes and impulses which in their undisguised and undistorted form would be repulsed by consciousness. The art-work and the Dream-Work employ identical mechanisms, and Freud describes the work of art as a public dream, and the dream as a private work of art. Aristotle employed the concept of *Catharsis* to describe the peculiar effect of tragedy on an audience. Catharsis is usually translated to mean the purgation of the emotion of pity and fear. The key term in this definition is purgation, a discharge of energy. Freud's view on the ultimate psychological value of art is similar to Aristotle's except that for him, Catharsis is the discharge of unconscious emotions.

"Jokes and Their Relation to the Unconscious" (1905)

The technique of jokes operates in a manner similar to the technique of the Dream-Work. Jokes employ the methods of condensation, displacement, allusion, substitution of a trivial idea for an important one; but, unlike dreams, jokes perform a social function, they require an audience. The source of all jokes, humor, wit and comedy is man's repressed instinctual nature, especially the instincts of sex and aggression. In civilization, these emotions (and all their variations) can seldom be expressed directly. But they are permitted entry into consciousness in the distorted form of jokes and humor, WHOSE TRUE UNCONSCIOUS MEANING is understood by all. Jokes allow a momentary suspension of the repressions which bind the emotions of forbidden sexuality and aggression, a discharge of the energy of the counter-cathexis which maintains the repressions, and the feeling of pleasure which accompanies this discharge.

A joke like a dream can be psychoanalyzed into its unconscious components; but then, of course, it is no longer a joke, a source of pleasure and discharge of repressed psychic energy, but rather another instance of how the systems *Pcs.* (Pre-conscious)-Ucs. (Unconscious) produce compromise-formations which momentarily lift the repressions guarding consciously forbidden material and at the same time disguise this forbidden material so that it becomes acceptable to consciousness.

Humor also acts as a defense-mechanism against unpleasure. It allows us to discharge energy that would normally deal directly with the source of unpleasure itself, energy supporting the repression of forbidden impulses PLUS the disguised forbidden impulses themselves. This process thus becomes a source of doubly heightened pleasure. As is the case with so many forms of adult behavior, jokes "take us back to the state of childhood." Jokes are the adult version of the child's fondness for playing with words as if they were things, real objects. The mastery of language itself produces pleasure. (The colloquial phrase "play on words" suggests the intimate connection between words and pleasure.)

We know how severely repressed the instincts of sexuality and aggression are in civilized men. Jokes rank high among the Substitute-Gratifications which civilization permits, allowing us to momentarily overcome these repressions and

experience, in verbal fantasy, uninhibited sexual-aggressive
pleasure of a kind that would never be permitted in reality.

"Leonardo da Vinci:
A Study in Psychosexuality" (1910)

In the year 1910, Freud wrote the first classic in the es-
thetics of Psychoanalysis, the Leonardo book, which he described as "... the only pretty thing I have ever written."
This work possesses a unique fascination for the student of
Freud's mind and the science of Psychoanalysis. *First,* its in-
herent content, the life of one of the greatest and most mysterious "universal-geniuses" in the history of humanity,
captures the interest of the student. *Second,* it is the very
first psychoanalytic biography. It opened an entirely novel
area of investigation to the fledgling science. *Third,* and
perhaps most important of all, was Freud's fascination
with Leonardo's personality. Ernest Jones observes that
the person of Leonardo exercised a profound fascination
for Freud. There was perhaps an unconscious identification on Freud's part, not so much with the personal life of
the Renaissance master, but rather with the central problem of his life as Freud saw it. This problem may be
phrased thus: What happens to the impulse to investigate
nature, the inborn curiosity of children in the process of
maturation, and what unconscious connections can be uncovered linking the artistic and scientific activities of mankind? Freud claimed that biographers are attracted to their
subject matter by certain unconscious affinities which the
author shares with his subject. Perhaps such an affinity
may be discovered in Freud's attraction to the personality
of Leonardo as the subject matter of the first psychoanalytic biography.

Freud's Thesis on Leonardo

In our discussion of *Moses and Monotheism,* we employed the analogy of a writer of detective stories in order
to clarify Freud's methodology. The detective metaphor is

even more germane to the Leonardo monograph. Freud carefully marshals a number of historically recorded events (clues) in the life of the great artist-scientist, events which produced a sense of mystery in his contemporaries. These events, taken independently by themselves, can certainly be explained in other ways than the Freudian. The question facing the student is whether Freud's attempt to connect and interpret these events psychoanalytically admits of no other explanation.

Freud builds his case on the following well-known events of Leonardo's life:

1. While many of his contemporaries in fifteenth-sixteenth century Italy were prolific painters and sculptors, his own output was meagre. He left a number of unfinished works and was extremely careless in painting the famous *Last Supper* on a limestone wall in fresco, a technique which to all intents and purposes has destroyed the original.

2. Leonardo's scientific investigations began to interfere with, then finally replace his artistic output.

3. He was something of a dilettante, wasting much creative effort in the service of producing frivolous pastimes for the court of the Duke of Milan: games, pageants, masqes, etc., mere playthings to a man of genius.

4. He was gifted not only as an artist, but as a practical man of science and engineering as well. A letter survives which Leonardo wrote Cesare Borgia, a condottiere who sought to unite all of Italy in the fifteenth century, in which he offers his services as a military engineer, describing a wide variety of weapons, military devices and techniques he could supply the ambitious Borgia.

5. He was fascinated by the phenomenon of flight. He sketched and designed some early flying machines.

6. He was left-handed and wrote his notebooks in front of a mirror so that they could not be easily deciphered.

7. Though an extremely handsome and powerful man (he could bend horseshoes with his bare hands), he was never know to have taken a mistress; this in an era of complete licentiousness.

8. He had the habit of buying caged birds, intended for sacrifice, and setting them free.

9. He surrounded himself in his atelier with strikingly handsome boys as pupils. None of these pupils ever amounted to much as an artist.

10. In his youth he was charged, with his master Verrocchio, of committing sodomy (homosexual-anal intercourse). He was exonerated of the charge.

Although these specific and seemingly unrelated events in the life of a great man might spark the curiosity of any investigator, the impetus to Freud's investigation was supplied from other sources. One of these sources was Leonardo's "Vulture Fantasy." Another was the dictum reported in his notebooks concerning the study of nature, "No one can either love or hate anything until he understands it." Still another motivation, popularity of what may be the single most famous painting in the world, Leonardo's "Mona Lisa."

In his journals Leonardo recorded that his earliest memory from infancy was of a peculiar event that had impressed itself with singular force on his psyche, an event which seemed prophetic of his nature. He "recollected" that, as an infant in his cradle, a vulture had flown in the window of his room, perched on the edge of his cradle, and tapped him several times on the mouth with its tail. With this memory-fantasy begins one of the most fascinating pieces of psychoanalytic detective work that the science has yet produced.

It must be borne in mind that Freud is handling the evidence presented him by Leonardo's biographer Giorgio Vasari and from Leonardo's own journals in the same way a psychoanalyst would treat events related to him by a patient. Freud is literally psychoanalyzing Leonardo. In one sense this procedure of Freud's is illegitimate from the

psychoanalytic point of view. In discussing the interpretation of symbols in therapy, Freud held that the patient must
supply the associations and that the analyst could not understand the nature of the case before him through the use
of symbolic interpretations alone. On the other hand, Leonardo has "spoken" to his analyst in a number of significantly personal ways, as we shall shortly see.

But in addition to the fascinating analysis of Leonardo,
the man and artist, Freud writes some profoundly important pages for any student of science and philosophical investigation. In no other work does Freud so neatly conjoin
unconscious impulses with the conscious drive to investigate
and understand nature.

Leonardo's "Memory" as Fantasy

Leonardo's vulture "memory" Freud treats as a vulture
"fantasy," arguing that it is highly improbable that a vulture would appear on the plains of Tuscany in Northern
Italy and then proceed to fly into an infant's room, perch
on his cradle and tap his mouth with its tail. Freud interpreted this event as a SCREEN-MEMORY which, it will be
recalled from the discussion of Hysteria, is not a genuine
memory at all but rather a fantasy which disguises a wish.
The first criticism levelled at Freud's interpretation of the
vulture was the rather carping one that the Italian noun
"nibbia" does not mean vulture at all. Nibbia means kite
(the bird, not the toy). Whatever the ornithological differences between kite and vulture may be, psychoanalytically
speaking, it would make no difference to the Freudian symbolic interpretation if a canary had flown into the infant
Leonardo's room. It is the symbolic significance of the bird
that is under investigation here.

In Psychoanalysis, a bird of any kind is universally symbolic of the MALE SEX ORGAN, THE PHALLUS. Not
only in dreams is this discovered to be the case, but vulgar
linguistic usage confirms the unconscious equation bird-

phallus. In German, Freud writes, the term *vöglein,* to bird, refers euphemistically to sexual intercourse. Had he been so inclined, Freud might have found a number of such linguistic connections. In English, it is quite well known that the term "cock" has the double meaning of bird and phallus. The same is true in Greek, Swahili, and Tibetan, to cite a number of wide-spread instances. Leonardo's screen-memory thus can be seen to represent a disguised infantile wish-fulfillment dealing not at all with birds but with sexual matters.

Revealing the nature of this fantasy of Leonardo's once again brought down the wrath of Freud's contemporaries on his head, for Freud argued that the vulture-fantasy gives a strong indication of unconscious homosexual tendencies in the great man.

Leonardo's Childhood

It is well known that Leonardo was the bastard child of Sr. Pietro da Vinci and a peasant girl whose name was Katerina. The infant son was left in his mother's care exclusively during the formative years of infancy and childhood; then, adopted by his natural father. The psychoanalytic investigation of homosexuals reveals two universal occurrences. First, the homosexual's mother is often the dominant parent; but if this is not literally the case, she is the parent with whom the little boy identifies. Often, she raises her male child alone, in the absence of the father. Second, in the analysis of homosexuals, Freud found the unconscious symbolic equation: PHALLUS-BREAST! The role of the phallus in homosexual deviation symbolically replaces the longed-for maternal breast.

Psychogenesis of Homosexuality

Freud here comes to grips with the psychogenesis of homosexuality, rejecting the idea that the homosexual belongs to a so-called "third sex," arguing that the normal male child is MADE INTO A HOMOSEXUAL BY HIS MOTH-ER! Freud hypothesized that the abandoned Katerina show-ered excessive libidinal love upon her infant son to com-pensate for the love denied her by her aristocratic lover. As is the case with most mothers of homosexuals, they seek libidinal compensation from their sons, though quite uncon-sciously, for the mature masculine love of which they are deprived for one reason or another, and their behavior is devastatingly seductive to the yet unformed infant's Ego. THEY UNCONSCIOUSLY SEDUCE THEIR SONS INTO BECOMING HOMOSEXUALS. It is the seductive mother who prevents the male homosexual from loving other wom-en and developing into a normal heterosexual male. The ho-mosexual male, deprived of a masculine father-figure with which to identify, and sexually seduced by a love-starved mother, remains true to her by renouncing his psychosexual maturity.

Several of the events in Leonardo's biography become clear if Freud's speculations are correct. The Vulture screen-memory is actually the unconscious infantile wish for the maternal breast, the most sexually gratifying object Leonardo had ever known. His total indifference to women (indeed, his horror of women), the collection of pretty boy apprentices which filled his workshop, the charges of sod-omy with Verrocchio, and his preoccupation with the phe-nomenon of flight (unconscious meaning: sexuality) and birds (unconscious meaning: phallus-maternal breast) be-gin to assume the form of a meaningful psychoanalytic pattern.

The problem which has fascinated critics and laymen alike is the nature of the universally recognized seductive-ness of the Mona Lisa "smile." Hundreds of thousands of Americans viewed this picture when on loan recently from the Louvre. An extremely popular song dealing with the subject was recorded by the late Nat King Cole and a well-known Charles Adams' cartoon in *New Yorker* magazine deals with the enigmatic and macabre nature of the smile.

These instances are presented to suggest that the problem of the Mona Lisa smile extends far beyond the traditional boundaries of artistic criticism. Perhaps no other work of art is so well-known by so many human beings as Leonardo's "Mona Lisa." Leonardo painted the Mona Lisa (technically named *La Gioconda*) at the very end of his life and it was one of the few possessions he took with him when he became court painter to King Francis I of France. WHAT IS THE SOURCE OF MANKIND'S UNIVERSAL ENCHANTMENT WITH THE MONA LISA SMILE?

Bifurcation of Love and the Mother

In a series of essays dealing with the Psychology of Love, written between 1912-1918, Freud analyzed and discussed what he thought to be the principal psychosexual problem confronting the human male. As we know, the male infant selects his mother as his first love-object and feels both *sensuality* and *tenderness* for her. It is the combination of the *SENSUAL AND TENDER ATTITUDES* which define human love for Freud. While the attitude of tenderness toward the mother is not only acceptable, but required, the sensuous feelings are forced to undergo repression. But these two emotional currents continue to seek reunification in the unconscious psychic life and in the adult heterosexual behavior of the male. This is the most difficult obstacle which each male child must in some manner overcome on the road to masculinity, the recombination of the tender and sensual attitudes toward a woman, which were severed in childhood. Needless to remark, it is a task which is seldom successfully completed. The bifurcation of the original libidinal unity is the cause of civilization's double sexual standards, and the degradation of one "kind" of woman (the sex-object, the whore) and elevation of another "kind" of woman (the mother-wife). The celebration of Mother's Day is a mawkish reminder of one side of this devastating split, while the pressure-cooker sexual fantasies of Playboy Magazine graphically illustrate the other side, the suppressed longings of millions of adult males. But, a nice boy does not take a Playboy Bunny home to meet his Mother! The two "kinds" of women are rigidly separated in both the psyche and the behavior of the average male.

Woman-Hating Men

Often the male whose libidinal currents have undergone very severe repression will entirely eschew the sensual attitude toward women. He will find the female genitalia "disgusting," and be repelled by them. (Of course, strong elements of unconscious castration-anxiety play a part.) Leonardo was one of these males. In his journals he describes the female genitalia as so disgusting that Nature was forced to invent pretty faces to attach to the female organs of reproduction otherwise the human race would long ago have ceased to exist! The fate of the sensuous current felt toward the mother in Leonardo was that it underwent such severe repression that he turned away from women altogether and became what Freud called an "ideal homosexual." By this he meant that Leonardo was probably not a practicing homosexual but that his psychosexual development had been arrested in infancy and split into two divergent streams, the tender and the sensual, and that he was forever prohibited from following the course of normal heterosexual development by the severe repression which his prematurely developed sexual atttitudes toward his mother must have undergone. Contrary to popular superstition, Freud wrote, the homosexual male IS sensuously attracted to women. But he is compelled to flee from this attraction in order to remain "faithful" to the tender, non-threatening image of the Mother. It is the tender, non-threatening (castration-anxiety) Mother who becomes the conscious object of her son's love, while the sensuous, threatening (provocative of castration-anxiety) Mother is repressed into the unconscious and her very existence denied. But, as Freud discovered, the unconscious memory of the sensuously provocative Mother survives in all males, and the attempt to re-unite the divided currents of sensuality and tenderness in relation to a mature love-object, a "real" woman, arouses all of the unconscious complexes and anxieties associated with the original object of a male child's sensuous-tender love, his mother.

"Mona Lisa's" Smile as Wish-Fulfillment

But in fantasy, the great artist possesses the power to resolve the most realistically insoluble conflicts. That again is the source of his power over an audience, the premium of pleasure which his genius enables us to acquire WITHOUT the accompanying anxieties which invariably gravitate about the tabooed subject matter of his art. The Mona Lisa perfectly accomplishes in fantasy, what is absolutely prohibited in reality, the complete fulfillment of an infantile wish-fantasy. The secret of the Mona Lisa smile lies in its ability to COMBINE THE SENSUOUS AND TENDER elements which the child first experiences at the Mother's breast, which is subsequently lost through repression, and recaptured in fantasy through the work of an artistic genius, Leonardo has "solved" mankind's insoluble psychological task. He painted the ultimate WISH-FULFILLMENT of all men.

The student should take note of the fact that Freud never believed that Psychoanalysis could explain "how" works of art are made. Civilized man's most perfectly developed psychic faculty, *Sublimation*, the capacity to convert sexual and aggressive energies into enduring social values, was forever beyond the ken of psychoanalytic comprehension. "... we have to admit ... that the nature of artistic attainment is psychoanalytically inacccessible to us." What Freud succeeded in doing in his work on Leonardo was reveal the nature of one of the enduring themes in art, the mysterious nature of Woman as captured in the Mona Lisa smile.

An addition to the Freudian theory is required. A further piece of confirmatory evidence was discovered which "clinches" the case, so to speak, that Leonardo's conscious preoccupation with the vulture theme was a distortion of his unconscious preoccupation with the part played by his mother in his psychosexual development. In another painting of Leonardo's, the *Holy Family,* which depicts St. Anne, the Virgin Mary and the infant Jesus, Freud's pupils Jung and Pfister DISCOVERED THE UNMISTAKABLE OUT-LINES OF A VULTURE IN THE GARMENTS OF THE VIRGIN! This picture may be seen and judged for oneself in Andre Malraux's *Voices of Silence* (page 3). If this picture is convincing, then it provides one of the most compelling pieces of evidence in confirmation of the Freudian theory!

But Freud ranged far beyond this discovery into the realm of philosophic discussion, raising issues which call into question the nature of the scientific *enterprise.*

Science, Art, and the Impulse to Investigate Nature

Evidently, Leonardo's scientific investigations first impeded and then finally brought to a halt his artistic work. The compulsion to investigate superseded the need to create. In a little noted section of the Leonardo monograph Freud inquires into the origin and fate of scientific and philosophic curiosity and relates it to the period of infantile sexual investigation. The "highest" things in human culture are shown to have their origins in the "lowest," that is, scientific investigation and artistic creation spring from identical roots in infantile sexual curiosity Freud discovered that children actually develop substantial theories concerning birth and sexual differentiation, and that this infantile activity becomes sublimated in humanity's most far-reaching theories on the origins and nature of reality. The most abstruse theorizing of an Einstein is grounded in the identical impulse which leads a little child to ask the universal question, "Where do babies come from?" Curiosity about the universe is grounded in infantile sexual curiosity!

Sexual curiosity in infants is usually severely repressed. Either they are told fabulous tales of the stork (significantly, a bird!) bringing them, or they are discouraged from further enquiry by threats. The repression of the sexual curiosity of the young accompanies the repression of their first attempts at sexual experience, the two activities are repressed together. The repression of the sexual impulses includes the repression of the investigatory impulse and, as Freud writes, "... the free activity of intelligence may be narrowed for life." This is the fate of most human beings. Their natural curiosity suffers the same fate as their natural sexuality. It is repressed, distorted, and in many cases destroyed altogether.

There is a second potential result of sexual repression in relation to the investigatory impulse. The sexual impulses are not completely subjugated but the investigatory impulse returns to adult consciousness in the form of COMPULSIVE REASONING WHICH IS A SUBSTITUTE FOR FORBIDDEN SEXUAL QUESTIONS! Such reasoning goes round and round and never arrives at a conclusion, because it is unconsciously forbidden to do so! To arrive at a conclusion of compulsive reasoning would be to arrive at the forbidden answer to sexual questions! Much systematic philosophy, according to Freud, is of just this nature.

The third outcome of the dual process of sexual-investigatory repression, one which Freud attributed to the case of Leonardo (and in all probability we can attribute it to Freud's life as well; this fact would provide the unconscious link which bound these two great minds together), he described in the following words: "... the libido withdraws from the fate of the repression by being sublimated from the outset into curiosity, and by reinforcing the powerful investigatory impulse." Investigation REPLACES SEXUAL ACTIVITY; hence, is excepted from the fate of sexuality, i.e., is not repressed. All aspects of the philosophic and scientific investigator's erotic life are subject to SUB-LIMATION AND UNDERSTANDING in place of direct gratification. This is the psychoanalytic explanation of Leonardo's dictum that one cannot either love or hate anything until one has understood it. Freud argues that the withholding of libidinal energy from anything (anyone) until it is understood severely impairs both the capacity to love and hate. And this is exactly the unconscious purpose of such restrictions, by witholding libido, it is dissipated in the very process of investigation. INVESTIGATION REPLACES AND BECOMES A SUBSTITUTE FOR LIBIDINAL GRATIFICATION!

In Leonardo's biography, this process is perfectly exemplified. Slowly the artist was replaced by the investigator and the investigatory impulse finally submerges the artistic. Leonardo defended himself against libidinal erotic-creative FORBIDDEN impulses, by INVESTIGATING AND THROUGH THE PROCESS OF INVESTIGATING, DESTROYED THEM!

It was not until AFTER THE DEATH OF BOTH HIS FATHER AND MOTHER that Leonardo was able to paint the Mona Lisa. In his journals, he reveals the profound unconscious importance these events had for him as for all men. We know that mistakes of any kind reveal unconscious conflicts of great magnitude. We know also that the death of a man's father is the most important event in his life. Leonardo, a usually scrupulous man in the keeping of household accounts, MADE DOUBLE ENTRIES FOR THE FUNERAL EXPENSES OF BOTH HIS FATHER AND MOTHER! These double entries reveal how profoundly important these events were in Leonardo's unconscious. The Mona Lisa was painted after the death of his parents, as if it represented a regressive return in fantasy to his deepest childhood wishes, the deepest childhood wishes of all men. Leonardo's libido had been finally liberated from bondage to investigation!

Reaction to "Leonardo"

The Leonardo book was received "with horror," and a general misapprehension of the purpose of the psychoanalytic theory of art was firmly established among its opponents. Among the criticisms directed at Freud's theory were:

1. The enjoyment and value of an art work is destroyed by analyzing it into its unconscious components. Freud murdered to dissect!

2. The great artist is reduced to a mere neurotic, like the rest of us. His work becomes a symptom of his sickness.

Freud, who shared Leonardo's intellectual passion, was certain that understanding a work of art, from any perspective, enhanced its value. Knowledge is a natural pleasure and all men naturally desire to know (Aristotle's first epistemological principle). Psychoanalytic criticism no more "destroyed" the value of a great work of art than did any other kind of criticism. Indeed, it enhanced the pleasure produced by great art works, by revealing a novel dimension of human experience in which both the artist and his audience participated; it supplied the unconscious link between the two.

The second criticism was expressly rejected by Freud. The great artist is first and foremost a human being, and like the rest of humanity in sharing the same universal conflicts and sufferings. This proposition merely places the artist within a human frame of reference. But he differs from the rest of humanity in that he possesses the unique ability to transmute his unconscious conflicts, shared with the rest of us, into an enduring source of value and enlightenment.

The remainder of the unaccounted for peculiarities in Leonardo's biography Freud interprets in the following manner:

His meagre output and the number of works he left unfinished can be understood as Leonardo's unconscious attitude toward his spiritual "children" his paintings. He treated them in exactly the same way as his father had treated him, by leaving them unfinished as his father had left him "unfinished," i.e., a homosexual.

Also the investigatory impulse enabled Leonardo to sublimate the urge to paint. The restraint he exercised in order to understand better anything before loving or hating (or painting) it was highly detrimental to his emotional capacities. Such restraint ultimately results in understanding *replacing* loving, hating and painting! SCIENTIFIC INVESTIGATION REPLACED BOTH EROTIC RELATIONSHIPS AND THE URGE TO PAINT!

The childish "waste of time" which dissipated so much of his energies and which was a source of reproach by his contemporaries, Freud explained by the necessary unconscious survival of much of the infantile mental life in a man of genius. The genius "plays" with reality and is dominated by the Primary Process and the realm of unconscious fantasy.

Leonardo's left-handedness suggested a biological basis for the homosexual elements in his personality. The left-side of the human body symbolizes the female half of the personality.

His interest in things military suggests a suppressed vein of sadistic cruelty in the great man. Leonardo would follow criminals to execution in order to sketch their facial expressions. He was as fascinated by ugliness as by beauty.

Addendum: What is the Reason for the Vehement Objections to Freud's Work?

In May 1926 on the occasion of his seventieth birthday, Freud was heartily congratulated by his pupils and colleagues on the "victory" Psychoanalysis had won from a grudging world. For the first time in the history of Vienna, post-offices were kept open on Sunday in order to handle the volumes of birthday mail pouring into the city, a most remarkable fact when we consider that Freud was a Jew living in a Catholic and anti-Semitic country. (Hitler got his start in Vienna!) Freud was unconvinced. He was not taken in by humanity's apparent acceptance of Psychoanalysis. Don't be misled, he told his pupils. The world has adopted Psychoanalysis in ORDER TO BE BETTER ABLE TO DESTROY IT!

In the "years of splendid isolation," when he alone nurtured the truths of Psychoanalysis, Freud had slowly and painfully become aware that the world does not thank those who disturb its slumbers, especially in the discomforting area of human sexual behavior. It was the clinical discovery of the RESISTANCES that enabled Freud to finally comprehend the nature of the attacks upon Psychoanalysis, which more often than not, took the form of attacks against him personally.

The human race collectively responded to his discoveries in the exact manner of a patient in therapy. Freud distinguished between the neurotic defensive Resistance to his discoveries and rational criticism. True, he insisted that a critic of Psychoanalysis was ony qualified if he had undergone the experience of being analyzed. But this certainly means no more than arguing that no one has the critical right to dispute a physician's diagnosis of an ailment if he knows nothing of the theory and practice of medicine or a mechanic's judgment of the malfunction of an auto engine if he knows nothing of the workings of the internal combustion engine.

Some Critical Reactions to Freud's Discoveries

The following is a very partial sampling of Resistances, not rational criticisms of Psychoanalysis. They are a very small selection from a truly voluminous literature.

THE INTERPRETATION OF DREAMS

It took eight years to sell just 600 copies of this scientific classic. After 18 months, not a single scientific journal had reviewed it. An assistant at the Psychiatric Clinic (Vienna) wrote a book disproving Freud's theories NEVER HAVING READ *THE INTERPRETATION OF DREAMS!* He was informed by his colleagues that it was not worth the effort.

One critic suggested in a public lecture that Freud had constructed his theory in order to "fill his pockets adequately."

Another described *The Interpretation of Dreams* as "complete mysticism and chaotic arbitrariness."

Still another wrote that in this work "the imaginative thoughts of an artist had triumphed over the scientific investigator."

And over a quarter century after its publication, *The Interpretation of Dreams* was described as another of "the well-known dream books, printed on bad paper (!) which may be found in cook's drawers."

TOTEM AND TABOO

Ernest Jones writes "Outside of analytic circles, the book met with total disbelief as one more personal fantasy of Freud's."

LEONARDO DA VINCI

A friend wrote at length to Freud describing the "horror" that this book evoked among well-meaning people.

THREE ESSAYS ON THE THEORY OF SEXUALITY

Jones quotes a critic who said that "Freud was a man with an evil and obscene mind."

THE FUTURE OF AN ILLUSION

Freud had no right to intrude in an area of specialization not his own.

MOSES AND MONOTHEISM

Freud had no right to opinions on the topics dealt with until he had mastered Hebrew, Egyptian and other Mid-Eastern languages. His writing was motivated by a *bitter hatred of the Jews!*

He resembled a fanatical Christian, wrote another critic, in his *hatred of Israel!*

He was begged by one Jewish scholar not to publish the book.

It was widely broadcast that Ernest Sellin, the biblical scholar who first proposed the Moses-murder theory, repudiated it at a later date. Dr. Jones' research proved that not only was there no evidence for Sellin's recantation; on the contrary, he argued that he had discovered further confirmation in biblical traditions for it.

The subsequent history of Psychoanalysis confirmed Freud in his conviction that sexuality was the single, most intolerable subject matter confronting human understanding.

The majority of Freud's pupils not only broke with him personally, but developed their own versions of "Psychoanalysis." Adler, Jung, Rank and many others including the Neo-Freudians Horney, Fromm and Sullivan, de-emphasized, diluted and finally destroyed altogether the very heart of Freud's theories of the neuroses by denying the key etiological role of sexuality, the unconscious and the instinct theory. Psychoanalysis was made socially acceptable through emasculation. Freud's "nasty" theories of sexuality were scrubbed up and presented to a grateful world as "Psychoanalysis," which they most certainly are not. The world has accepted Psychoanalysis in its contemporary distortions. But it is no longer Freud's science of mind. The principles of that science are to be found in Freud and Freud alone. Hopefully this study guide has succeeded in a clear and accurate exposition of those principles.

STUDY QUESTIONS

If the student can satisfactorily answer the following questions, he has acquired a good, general knowledge of Freud's theories. But we wish to reiterate that this study guide IS NO SUBSTITUTE for a first-hand comprehension in depth of Freud's writings.

1. What is meant by the term conversion hysteria? Precisely WHAT is in the process of "being converted" in this neurosis?

2. Differentiate *Totem* from *Taboo*. How are they related? Where does Freud derive his evidence for the theory of the Primal Horde?

3. What does Freud mean by "Polymorphous Perverse"? How are perversions related to neurosis? How are both related to *normal* psychology?

4. What is the Dream-Work? How is the Latent Dream related to the Manifest Dream?

5. What are the major techniques employed by the Censor in the formation of dreams?

6. Why did Freud find Hypnosis unsatisfactory as a therapeutic technique? What replaced it? What was the crucial difference in the two methods?

7. What did Freud mean by "psychosexual stages of development"? How does the Freudian theory of human sexuality differ from commonly accepted theories?

8. What constitutes the crucial differences in the psychosexual development of men and women?

9. Why does Freud characterize the Unconscious as the "Kingdom of the Illogical"?

10. Define *Repression, Resistance, Regression.* Why is the *Transference* situation such an obstacle to successful therapy?

11. How are dreams related to primitive languages?

12. On what grounds does Freud assert that Psychoanalysis is a "science"?

13. What evidence does Freud present for his assertion that Moses was an Egyptian? How does the "Moses" thesis relate to the Primal Horde theory in explaining both Jewish consciousness and anti-Semitism?

14. How does the psychoanalytic theory of art "explain" both the life and work of Leonardo da Vinci? Why is the Mona Lisa so popular?

15. Why is human happiness impossible in civilization?

16. How does the Death Instinct theory modify all of Freud's earlier convictions on the nature of the instincts?

17. In its final formulation, how are the Ego, Id and Super-Ego defined and related to one another? What does Freud mean by Dynamic, Economic and Topographical in relation to these three mental qualities?

18. What is meant by the assertion that Freud is a "dualist"?

19. What is Ambivalence and why is it so important in Freudian theory?

20. Describe Fechner's Principle of Constancy.

21. What is meant by the *Freudian Principle of the Continuity* of all mental events?

22. Why are all manifestations of human behavior "Compromise-Formations"?

23. How are infantile frustrations and traumas related to adult neurotic disorders?

24. What were the three "clues" which indicated the importance of disturbed sexuality in mental disorders?

25. Why is religion an "illusion"?

26. What is the relationship which exists between the leader and the members of any group?

27. In what way do totemic elements survive in more sophisticated religions?

28. When is "cure" achieved in Psychoanalysis?

29. What are the major difficulties encountered in psychoanalytic therapy?

30. What is the Oedipus Complex? How does it differ in men and women?

31. "Where" (i.e., in what area or agency of the mental personality) does the function of "repression" occur?

32. What does Freud mean by Ego-Syntonic?

33. What is Lay Analysis?

34. Distinguish the meanings of the terms Psychology, Psychiatry, Psychotherapy and Psychoanalysis.

35. What is the Primary Process? Why is it so important a part of the theory of Psychoanalysis?

36. How are the *Repetition Compulsion* and the *Return of the Repressed* related?

37. Define Cathexis and Abreaction.

38. What is the Scientific Weltanschauung? How is Psychoanalysis included within the meaning of this term?

39. Distinguish between "bound" and "tonic" energy.

40. What does Freud mean by the "psychic economy"?

GLOSSARY OF PRINCIPAL FREUDIAN TERMS

Abreaction (Catharsis): The discharge of psycho-biological energy, especially in therapy associated with the recollection of repressed ideas and impulses.

Ambivalence: The holding of absolutely opposed psychological attitudes (primarily love and hate) directed toward the same object (person). This is the fundamental emotional attitude in all human beings.

Cathexis: A charge of psycho-biological energy connected to ideas, impulses, wishes, feelings.

Compromise-Formation: The manifestations of human behavior which combine unconscious, forbidden impulses with conscious forces of repression. ALL HUMAN BEHAVIOR IS IN THE NATURE OF A COMPROMISE-FORMATION.

Condensation: The process by which a multitude of latent unconscious dream-thoughts are represented as a single element in the Manifest Dream.

Death Instinct: Freud's final theory on the nature of the instincts. This instinct is primary in all living organisms, more fundamental than Eros, the life instinct, and represents the wish on the part of living protoplasm to return to an inorganic state free of biological tensions. Its derivatives are aggression, sadism and masochism.

Displacement: The major form of disguise-distortion censorship. What is genuinely important in the unconscious is represented as trivial in the conscious dream and vice versa. Displacement of both ideas AND emotions may occur in the Manifest Dream.

Dream-Work: The activity which preserves sleep by censoring and distorting unconscious wishes and permitting them hallucinatory gratification in the dream.

Ego, Id, Super-Ego: The Ego is what popular psychology generally identifies as the personality. It is the conscious portion of human psychology (although the entire Ego is not conscious, part of it suffers repression and becomes unconscious). It is the "reality-testing" mechanism. The Id is the instinctual Unconscious. It is the source of all instinctual energies. The Ego develops out of the Id. It is the most organized portion of the Id. Its function is to mediate between the instinctual demands of the Id and the requirements of the external world. The Super-Ego represents the survival of parental attitudes in the psyche and their incorporation in what is colloquially termed conscience. But the Super-Ego is for the most part unconscious. It is the source of guilt felt by the Ego for unconscious instinctual wishes.

Ego-Syntonic: Impulses, wishes, energies, ideas, etc., which are compatible with the conscious structure of the Ego.

Erogenous Zones: Any part of the human body which provides pleasure. Mouth, Anus, etc.

Eros: The most highly sublimated form of Libido. Eros is the source of the cohesiveness of social groups and all the higher cultural products of the human mentality.

Etiology: Cause.

Fixation: The libido remains at a pre-genital stage of psychosexual development and fails to achieve maturity. Oral-Anal-Phallic stages are pre-genital, that is, these zones of the body usurp the place of the more mature organs of sexual pleasure, the adult genitalia, and the function of reproduction.

Free Association: The process through which unconscious ideas are recollected in consciousness. It requires the total suspension of all conscious, rational, critical and moral faculties. The patient must tell the analyst anything that comes into his mind (Analytic Compact), no matter how seemingly irrelevant, repulsive or nonsensical. The first "free" association will invariably lead to a chain of associations which uncover the hidden thought or impulse.

Instinct (Trieb): An inborn quantity of energy differentiated into various functions, sexual, aggressive, narcissistic, etc. Instincts represent mankind's evolutionary biological heritage from its animal past.

Latent Dream: The unconscious (real) meaning of the Manifest Dream. The Dream-Work converts the Latent Dream-Thoughts.

Lay Analysis: The therapeutic practice of Psychoanalysis by non-medical persons. Freud argued that a medical degree was not requisite to the practice of the mental science of Psychoanalysis.

Libido: Sexual energy.

Manifest Dream: What is actually dreamt.

Metapsychology: A complete, comprehensive, definitive theory of human mental behavior. A total explanation of human psychology.

Oedipus Complex: The kernel of every neurosis. The universal psychological condition (repressed and unconscious in adults) in which the male infant loves and sexually desires his mother, hates his father and wishes to remove him as a rival for his mother's love. The reverse is true in the case of the female infant. She loves her father sexually and views her mother as a rival.

Parapraxes: Errors, forgetting, slips of the tongue. Any relatively unimportant and unnoticed piece of behavior which reveals important unconscious tendencies.

Pleasure Principle: The dominant law of human psychology, the universal and unending search for instinctual satisfaction.

Polymorphous Perverse: Infantile Sexuality. No moral judgment is implied. Polymorphous means *many-formed* and Perverse means *turned from its natural direction.* Infantile sexuality is not yet organized under the supremacy of genitality in the service of reproduction. It finds "sexual" pleasure in all zones of the body and all activities which, if carried-over into adulthood, become perversions in the literal sense.

Primary Process: Freud's term for the dynamics of the Unconscious, suggesting that unconscious mental activity is far more important than consciousness.

Reality Principle: The repressive forces of society-civilization which produces severe modifications of the Pleasure Principle.

Regression: The return of the libido to an earlier stage of psychosexual organization.

Repetition Compulsion: The neurotic, unconscious need to repeat traumatic experiences in order to gain control over them.

Repression: The activity initiated in the Ego which either prevents unconscious impulses from reaching consciousness, or so distorts and disguises them that they are acceptable to consciousness. Repression is the dynamic source of neurosis.

Resistance: Defense mechanisms set up by the repressed portion of the Ego. The Resistances seek to maintain the psychic status quo by preventing unconscious impulses, wishes and memories from coming into consciousness, thus causing painful anxieties associated with repressed complexes from reaching the threshold of awareness.

Return of the Repressed: The collective historical form of the Repetion Compulsion. Traumatic events in the history of the human race tend to be repeated in an attempt to gain control over them.

Sublimation: Civilized man's most highly developed psychic capacity. Sexual energy is deflected from direct gratification (aim-inhibited) and enlisted in the service of civilization, religion, morality, art, etc.

Symbolism: An inherited, unconscious capacity. The use of symbols disguises the unconscious, forbidden dream-thoughts and allows them access to consciousness. The activity of symbolism is universal in dreams, myths, poetry, fairy-tales and vulgar speech. Symbolism in dreams is primarily sexual.

Taboo: The unquestioned interdiction of certain activities, in primitive and civilized communities as well. Incest and the killing of the totem animal are the foremost taboos.

"Tonic" and "Bound" Energy: The first term refers to free-floating energy in the psychic systems which may be the cause of anxiety. The second term refers to the incorporation of this free-floating energy within the totality of the mental personality.

Totemism: The earliest form of religious organization. The worship of an animal as ancestor of a clan and the concomitant moral prohibitions.

Transference: In therapy, the unconscious "transferring" of infantile emotions from the patient's parents to the person of the analyst who thus becomes a surrogate parent. The Positive stage of Transference includes all the positive libidinal emotions, the patient "falls in love" with the analyst. The Negative Transference occurs when the patient begins to "hate" the analyst, as he hated the parent, for frustrating his sexual overtures. The Counter-Transference takes place if the analyst's own unconscious attitudes respond to the unconscious attitudes of the patient, that is, if the analyst begins to "love" or "hate" his patient.

Trauma: Greek for wound. The infantile experiences which establish the grounds for later adult neuroses (traumatic experiences).

Weltanschauung: A world-philosophy or world-view.

BIBLIOGRAPHY

Good, inexpensive editions of Freud's major works are available in a number of paperback publications. The editions listed below are those referred to in this text.

NORTON PUBLISHING CO.

Civilization and Its Discontents
The Ego and the Id
Jokes and Their Relation to the Unconscious
New Introductory Lectures in Psychoanalysis
Outline of Psychoanalysis
Totem and Taboo
The Question of Lay Analysis
The Problem of Anxiety
The Psychopathology of Everyday Life

VINTAGE BOOKS

Moses and Monotheism
Leonardo da Vinci: A Study in Psychosexuality

BANTAM EDITIONS

Beyond the Pleasure Principle
Group Psychology and the Analysis of the Ego

WASHINGTON SQUARE PRESS

A General Introduction to Psychoanalysis

ANCHOR BOOKS (DOUBLEDAY)

The Future of an Illusion

AVON

Three Essays on the Theory of Sexuality

The most definitive editions of *Studies in Hysteria* and the *Interpretation of Dreams* will be found in hard-cover editions published by *Basic Books Inc.* Freud's *Collected Papers* in 5 Volumes is published by the Hogarth Press.

The United States Department of Health, Education and Welfare recently published the *Abstracts of the Standard Edition of the Complete Psychological Works of Sigmund Freud,* edited by Carrie Lee Rothgeb, chief of the Technical Information Section of the National Clearinghouse for Mental Health Information. This compilation represents a complete and accurate condensation of all Freud's works as derived from the *Standard Edition of Freud,* edited by James Strachey. For the student interested in the total spectrum of Freud's writings, this Abstract may be obtained from the Supt. of Documents, U.S. Govt. Printing Office, Wash., D.C. 20402, Stock Number 1724-0139 ($1.75).

Freud's definitive biographer remains Dr. Ernest Jones. His 3-volume biography, *The Life and Work of Sigmund Freud* (Basic Books Inc.), remains unchallenged as a source of personal and scientific information for the serious student of Psychoanalysis. The one-volume edition, edited and abridged by Lionel Trilling and Steven Marcus with an introduction by Trilling, will suffice for the general reader.

NOTES

NOTES

NOTES

NOTES

NOTES

NOTES